MW01286414

GROWING MARIJUANA: A COMPREHENSIVE GUIDE

CANNABIS GROWING FROM SEED TO HARVEST INDOOR AND OUTDOOR

TERRY GORDON

© *Copyright 2019 by Terry Gordon / TGB Media Inc. - All rights reserved.*

This document is geared towards providing exact and reliable information regarding the subject covered. This publication is sold with the idea that the publisher is not required to render an accounting, officially permitted, or otherwise, of qualified services. If advice is necessary, legal or professional, a practiced individual in the profession should be ordered.

- From a Declaration of Principles which was accepted and approved equally by a Committee of the American Bar Association and a Committee of Publishers and Associations.

In no way is it legal to reproduce, duplicate, or transmit any part of this document in either electronic means or printed format. Recording of this publication is strictly prohibited and any storage of this document is not allowed unless with written permission from the publisher. All rights reserved.

The information provided herein is stated to be truthful and consistent, in that any liability, in terms of inattention or otherwise, by any usage or abuse of any policies, processes, or directions contained within is the solitary and utter responsibility of the recipient reader. Under no circumstances will any legal responsibility or blame be held against the publisher for any reparation, damages, or monetary loss due to the information herein, either directly or indirectly.

Respective authors own all copyrights not held by the publisher. The information herein is offered for informational purposes solely and is universal as so. The presentation of the information is without a contract or any type of guarantee assurance.

The trademarks that are used are without any consent, and the publication of the trademark is without permission or backing by the trademark owner. All trademarks and brands within this book are for clarifying purposes only and are the owned by the owners themselves, not affiliated with this document.

The information contained herein should not be construed as direct medical advice or recommendation. For medical advice, you should first consult your Physician.

Hello there my friend,

Thank you for purchasing my book. This comprehensive guide will thoroughly educate you on the many aspects of **Growing Marijuana**.

To add to your knowledge, I would like to offer you a free report that I'm sure you will find interesting. Simply click on the link below to access this **free report**:

"Healing with Herbs & Growing Your Own Herbs and Vegetables"

You will also be added to my advanced reading list group that makes you eligible to receive my upcoming new book releases prior to the launch date.

I would like to ask you for a favor. After you read this book, would you be kind enough to leave a review on Amazon? It would be greatly appreciated.

Click here to leave a review for this book on Amazon

Best regards,

Terry Gordon

TABLE OF CONTENTS

INTRODUCTION

Welcome to this guide on Growing Marijuana, your Comprehensive Guide to Cannabis Growing from Seed to Harvest Indoor and Outdoor.

This incredible guide will teach you step by step everything you need to start growing marijuana both indoors and outdoors. Discover how to avoid costly mistakes by following the information given in this guide. It will practically guarantee a flourishing crop right from your very first attempt.

Even if you've grown cannabis before you're still likely to learn from the useful tips and tricks contained on these pages.

The guide is split into two sections. The first details how to grow cannabis indoors and will show you how to set up your grow room and the optimum care and conditions requires to grow the best possible marijuana.

The second section is about growing cannabis outdoors and guides you through choosing the perfect location, right down to how to avoid pests and diseases, as well as how to take precautions with security.

Growing marijuana successfully can almost be considered an art form; it takes careful preparation, care and maintenance to successfully grow the perfect buds. Once you start seeing the fruits of your hard labor, growing can become something of a passion, even an obsession, growers always striving to improve things just a little bit to get a better crop each time.

It is important to note that marijuana is still illegal both to use and grow in many parts of the United States. Although gradually its amazing benefits as a medicine are being recognized so that more states are allowing the use of marijuana that has been prescribed by a medical professional, this is still not the case across all of America. The law on the legal use of marijuana both recreationally and medicinally are changing continually, so ensure you do your research and be careful to stay within the confines of the law where you live.

SECTION ONE – INDOOR GROWING

CHAPTER 1 - MARIJUANA CULTIVARS AND SEEDS

There are many differently named marijuana's available on the street, but in fact there are only three distinct species. These are:

• Indica

• Sativa

• Ruderalis

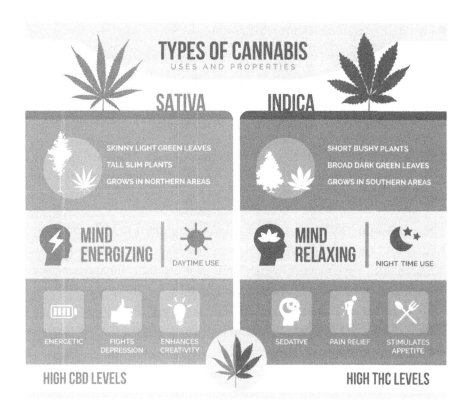

Indica is an annual, short stocky plant with a wide base, is densely branched and strong green in color. It is an ideal indoor growing plant. It has rounded leaves that feature a marbled leaf pattern.

Indica is believed to have originated in the Indus river basin area of Pakistan. This area is subjected to cold hard winters and warm summers, making this strain ideal for growers living in a temperate climate.

Indica is high in tetrahydrocannabinol (THC) and gives a heavy all over body stoned feeling making you very relaxed and often sleepy. It is the preferred species for medical uses as it has better pain-relieving properties than either of the other species.

- Pain relieving
- Muscle relaxing

- Can help to reduce seizures and spasms

- Provides migraine and headache relief

- Can aid restful sleep

- Can help reduce feelings of stress and anxiety

Sativa is an annual, which has a taller, less densely branched shape than Indica and is better suited to outdoor growing. The leaves are more open, with longer thinner points.

The seeds from the sativa type of cannabis are used to make hemp seed oil and for caged bird feed. The flowers (buds), leaves and stems contain cannabinoids, psychoactive compounds that are used for medical, recreational and spiritual purposes. Consumables for these purposes most commonly include hashish or oils for smoking, vaping or adding to edibles, but teas, tinctures and ointments can also be used.

Although sativa is used medicinally to treat mental illness and stress, more recent studies have shown that it can make psychiatric illness worse and can cause sleep disorders.

Like Indica, Sativa is high in THC, but gives a different kind of high, that is lighter and can increase creative thinking.

- Can help you feel at ease and give a sense of general wellbeing.

- Promotes cerebral thoughts that are uplifting.

- Energizes and stimulates

- Can help with creativity and increases focus

- Some strains can help to fight depression

Ruderalis is the smallest species of cannabis and it is rare for it to grow above 2 feet tall. The plant has a thin and somewhat fibrous stem with sparse branching. The leaves are large and open in form. Ruderalis matures faster than the other species of cannabis, usually taking between five to seven weeks from sowing.

Both Indus and Sativa rely on light cycles to reach the flowering stage, but Ruderalis does not, instead relying solely on the maturity of the plant. With Indica and Sativa varieties, it is possible to keep the plant in a permanent vegetative state by keeping the daylight cycle long, but Ruderalis will flower regardless of the number of daylight hours. This ability is called "auto-flowering" and it is a useful trait.

Ruderalis has a very low THC so is not generally cultivated for recreational purposes, but it does have a good cannabidiol (CBD) content, which makes it useful for medicinal uses. THC is what gives cannabis its ability to produce a psychotropic effect, but CBD has no psychotropic qualities.

Intervention by man has meant that the qualities of these three types of cannabis have been manipulated through careful inbreeding and crossbreeding to create plants that have the best qualities of all three types of cannabis, depending on the requirements of the grower and end user.

If a plant is required to be hardy and grow outdoors to produce an agricultural crop with virtually zero THC content, then a variety of Cannabis Sativa called Hemp is grown. If on the other hand a variety with high THC is required a hybrid of Sativa and Indus may be chosen

When growing cannabis for its psychoactive and medicinal properties it is common practice to separate the male and female plants. Plants sexes are separated to prevent pollination. Instead, pollen produced by the male plants can be stored until you require it.

When a female plant of one strain is pollinated by a male plant from a different strain the seeds that they produce will be F1 hybrids and will not be identical to the parent plants but have a mixture of both the plant's qualities and characteristics. Refinements can then be continued by cross breeding the plants with the better characteristics and so on; cubing is a common way of doing this. Cubing involves taking the F1 plants that have the characteristics most desired and then breeding them back to the parent plant that has specific qualities required. This can continue for three or more generations to produce plants exhibiting the best qualities.

The reason male and female plants are kept separated is because it is usual for the THC levels in female plants to rise when they are not pollinated. They will produce more flowers, buds and THC resin, thus producing plants with a better-quality harvest.

Doing your research and matching the inherent qualities of the plants you choose to grow to your needs and growing setup will maximize your satisfaction and potentially save you from making costly mistakes. There are many different varieties available. To begin with, talking to a specialist seed merchant about your requirements may be a good option. Seed merchants in Canada are your best option as marijuana is now legal across Canada. Alternatively, if you have a friend who is successfully growing marijuana with the properties you like, then ask for some seeds.

Check the quality of the seeds you receive, they should be dark brown with a marble pattern on them. This means the seeds are mature and are the ones most likely to germinate. If you receive seeds that are pale green, these are immature and will often not germinate.

Growing good marijuana is an art. Anyone can scatter a few seeds on the ground, but to make them flourish and grow to their optimum takes a bit more effort. However, the rewards make it well worth it.

TAKEAWAY

There are 3 species of cannabis plant Sativa, Indica and Ruderalis.

Most plants grown are hybrids of these three species.

Each species has its own individual qualities.

Sativa is tall growing and is high in psychoactive compounds, THC.

Promotes:

- Creative thinking

- Uplifted sense of wellbeing

- High energy levels

- Positivity

Indica is short and bushy it is also high in psychoactive compounds, THC

Promotes:

- Pain relief

- Muscle relaxation

- Seizure Control

- Headache and migraine relief

- Restful sleep

- Reduced feelings of stress and anxiety

Ruderalis is very small in size, it is also hardy and auto-flowering. It contains low levels of THC but is high in CBD.

CHAPTER 2 - GROW ROOM SETUP

For many, indoor growing is the only real option. If you decide indoor growing is the best option for you, check carefully before buying any seeds to ensure you're picking good varieties for this type of environment.

Seeds that are grown in optimum conditions will yield the best crops. How does over a pound per square meter sound? This is precisely why your grow room setup is of such vital importance. Lighting, temperature, humidity, and air circulation are all far more controllable when growing in an indoor environment. There will be no hailstorms or strong winds, and only a limited number of plant-eating insects, making it easier to keep your plants safe from harm.

Lighting

The right type of light is of paramount importance to your plants. They need light that works on the same spectrum as natural sunlight, as this is what they require to photosynthesize correctly. If a plant has insufficient light, then it can't create the sugars it requires to produce strong healthy plant tissue. The plant will be weak and prone to disease. As a guide, plants will need about 25 to 35 watts per square foot

There are two issues with lighting, expense and heat generation. It is these two reasons that make it important to choose the best type of lighting for you. There are several options available:

• Light Emitting Diode (LED)

• High Intensity Discharge Lamps (HIDs)

• Compact Fluorescent Lamps (CFLs)

LED lights have leapt forward in development in the past few years. They are without a doubt the best investment for an indoor grow room. The reason for this is threefold: they are versatile, very energy efficient and cool running. LEDs also have the ability to be made to produce different color spectra, this is very beneficial to plants as they require light of different wavelengths during different times of their growing cycle. By using specialist plant growing LEDs you can ensure your lighting is always perfect and help to maximize your plants yield. Depending on your budget you can opt for LEDs that offer an ultra-fine light adjustment within the color spectrum, or you can opt for more standard lights that offer a good ratio of both red and blue wavelengths.

Because they can last for 50,000 hours (12 hours per day for 10 years) or more, you will hardly ever have to replace the bulbs. Because they don't give off as much heat as other lighting you won't run the risk of overheating your plants, so can dispense with the added costs associated with installing cooling systems.

The top spec LED lights are pretty pricey to buy, but due to their assets, chances are they will save you a lot of money in the long run and give you the best possible results.

HIDs are now rather old-school and were what was used by indoor growers in the past. There are two types, metal halide (MH), and high-pressure sodium (HPS). MH lights produces blue spectrum light, which promotes plant growth, while the HPS lights give off an orange red light that increases hormone release and increases budding/flowering. HIDs are thirsty on power and operate at very high temperatures, which may not only overheat your plants but can be a fire hazard.

CFL lights that are produced specifically for indoor gardening are high powered fluorescents. They come in two types Blue 6400k for plant growth and Red 2700k for budding/flower growth. To get the best crops you will need to use both types, starting off with the blue and gradually changing to red until flowering.

They are a little less expensive to buy than LEDs but cost a lot more to run. They are also a little warmer than LEDs, but much cooler than HIDs.

Because at times it may be necessary to keep the lights on 24/7 to maximize potential growth, it's definitely the best option to go for LEDs.

Lights should be placed 20 to 30 inches from the top of the plant canopy. For this reason, installing a system where the lights can be lifted up and safely secured as the plants grow is a great idea.

If your budget won't stretch to LEDs, ensure that the lights you do use don't overheat your grow room and burn your plants' leaves. You can install a cooling system to help with this if necessary.

Ventilation

Regardless of the lights you opt for, ventilation is always going to be necessary. If there is a window that can be opened that's great. If that isn't practical, a fan system will need to be used to ensure there is fresh air circulation. Beware that cold air coming into the grow room can affect plant growth and may set your plants back, so only open a window if the temperature outside is favorable.

Temperature

Talking of temperature, it needs to be carefully monitored and regulated so that the room stays at an even 75 degrees Fahrenheit where possible. Although temperatures ranging a little above and below this will not cause too much harm, if there is too great a drop your plant won't produce high quality buds when it flowers. If temperatures get too high, the plants are prone to drying out. That means if you are using a room that is poorly insulated, investing in a good layer of insulation would be a wise thing to do. Insulation can give you a significant saving when it comes to keeping your grow room at an optimum temperature.

The best way to maintain even temperature is with the use of air conditioning units that can produce hot and cold air. If this isn't possible, setting the thermostat to the right temperature in the room will help, or use a heater with a thermostatic unit built in.

Humidity

Something novice growers often forget to think about is humidity. Humidity is simply water or dampness being held in the atmosphere. It can vary dramatically throughout the seasons and depending on where you live. Cannabis plants do well in a fairly wide range of humilities, with 40 to 80% relative humidity being acceptable. Humidity gauges are easy to buy and fairly accurate but controlling humidity can prove tricky. Dehumidifiers range in type, size and price quite dramatically, but by letting the room air through from time to time you should negate the need to buy anything too extravagant. One of the problems with humidity is that it can cause fungal diseases on the plants and these can be difficult to get rid of once they take hold.

Carbon Dioxide (CO2)

Marijuana needs CO_2 to grow and without enough of it, it won't thrive. You don't want so much CO_2 that you can't yourself breathe the air in the room, but you do want enough so your plants have a constant and plentiful supply. You can do this by getting a CO_2 generator that will keep your plants topped up and ensure they grow big beautiful buds.

Growing Mediums

A growing medium, which is also sometimes called a grow medium, is what the roots of your plant live in. This medium could be regular potting compost, perlite, coco coir, vermiculite, Rockwool or even water. The key to successful marijuana growing is to ensure that your plants roots have the perfect balance of nutrients, water, pH and oxygen, and this is what your growing medium must be able to provide.

1. Potting Compost or Soil

Using compost or soil is the most commonly used method to grow marijuana, simply because it is easy to get hold of and affordable.

The soil you choose needs to contain nutrients that can sustain your plant for the first few weeks of its life, without being too rich. The best soils to try are sterilized to ensure they are free from any disease, pests, bacteria or fungi. Loose non-peat potting compost is a good choice, especially an organic mix. Try to look for soils that have had perlite and soil conditioner added to them, as this improves drainage and helps increase airflow and oxygen at the roots to make the plants grow faster.

You can also use living composted soils, which have microorganisms living in them (rather like friendly gut bacteria in us). This type of soil is great for beginners as there is generally no need to add nutrients or change the pH of the water as living soils tend to remain well balanced themselves. These soils have another advantage, they produce strong buds with a highly aromatic scent and taste. Plants tend to grow a little slower in soil mediums than they do in other types.

2. Non-Soil Mediums

These types of potting mediums include:

• Perlite

- Coco coir

- Rockwool

- Vermiculite

- Peat Moss

- Calcined Diatomaceous Earth

Using one of these as your potting medium allows you to treat your plant similarly to if you were growing them in soil. The key difference is that all the plant's nutrient needs are given by you in the water through a hydroponic system. Because the plant's roots are receiving nutrients directly in this way, they grow a lot quicker and produce a greater yield than soil grown plants.

This system also helps prevent problems encountered with watering, as well as avoiding bugs that live in the soil.

Coco coir mixed with perlite is a favorite combination for this type of growing and setup is simple for even novice growers.

3. Hydroponics

As I explained in 2 above, plants can be contained in a pot with a soilless medium and fed hydroponically, adding the nutrients they need to the water you give them. However, this isn't true hydroponics. Hydroponics is really when you grow your cannabis with some of the roots sitting directly in the water at all times.

A good hydroponics setup will give you the fastest growth rates and the most control. Set up is fairly complex and can be costly, whether hydroponics is a good option for you depends what you are trying to achieve.

Setting up a hydroponics grow room is worthy of its own book, so I recommend reading more about it online to see if it is an option that would suit you.

Space

Overcrowding of your plants is not a good idea. It reduces airflow, which can cause problems with mildew, and the leaves won't be getting sufficient light. This ultimately will result in leggy plants putting all their growth into searching for light rather than producing lots of branches to produce buds.

That said however, they don't need too much space either. When you purchase your seeds, find out the general size the plant typically grows to. This should be a deciding factor in your purchase anyway. For indoor plants you want something that isn't too tall and that produces plenty of branches to carry buds. Remember that cannabis is a conical plant, so it is widest at its base tapering to the top.

The number of plants you can successfully grow will depend on the amount of space you have and the size each plant is anticipated to grow to. Using common sense is the best solution. You will soon see if the plants are getting over crowded, in which case it is better to thin them out.

Pots

You're going to need to grow your pot in pots (sorry I couldn't resist it). There are plenty of different types of suitable containers that you can use:

• Regular plastic or terracotta plant pots with saucers

• Hempy Buckets

• Smart pots

• Air pots

• Hydro

Regular plant pots are containers which have a hole or holes in the base to allow for drainage. They also usually have a saucer that they sit in to catch any excess water.

They are good because they are easy to find and are not expensive. The excess water that runs off can easily be thrown away or recycled.

Smart pots are made from fabric. They allow more oxygen to circulate around the roots of the plant and prevent the plant from becoming pot bound. Because they drain very freely and dry the growing medium out quickly, you will require a water holding additive to your soil – calcined (superheated) diatomaceous earth chips are ideal for this, as they soak up a lot of water and then release it gradually as the plant requires it. Very few other things have this ability. If you don't add a water holding additive, you will need to water plants in this type of pot more often. Also, because of the speed at which the medium dries in these pots, it is better to get a much larger size. A 5-gallon pot would be the smallest recommended size and would be equivalent to a 2-gallon regular pot.

Because smart pots don't come with a water saucer you will have to place them in something to catch water runoff.

Air Pots are very similar to Smart Pots and will allow lots of oxygen to the roots, but will require watering more regularly and a larger size of pot to be used along with a water retaining additive. The design of these pots is tall and thin, and this allows you to use a regular saucer to capture any water runoff.

Hempy Buckets are just like ordinary plant pots, except rather than having the holes in the base of the pot they are located at the sides close to the bottom. This allows for a small amount of water to collect at the bottom of the pot after watering and reduces the frequency watering is necessary. This can be advantageous as the plants grow and require more water. The downside to this is that if you over feed your plant nutrients, they can accumulate at the bottom of the container without getting washed out.

Workspace

When designing your grow room, try to keep practicality and ease of use in mind. If your plants are all close together and totally cover a large area you won't be able to tend to the plants in the middle very easily. Also think about where your plants will be placed, on the floor or on some kind of workbench.

Personally, I don't want to be bending down all the time to water and tend to my plants. I would rather they are raised a little off the floor somewhere between knee and hip height to make things easier. If you're going to use benches, make sure that they are really sturdy, can't be knocked over, and are waterproofed. I make the top of my workbench into one big water catching tray with several drainage holes that run off into buckets placed below the bench, this makes for easy management and quick cleanup.

TAKEAWAY

- The best type of lighting for a grow room is LED

- Plants require 25 to 35 watts of light per square foot

- Good ventilation is essential to create air flow and circulation

- Room temperature should be maintained at 75F

- Humidity should be kept between 40% and 80%

- CO_2 is required for the best plants, you can use a CO_2 generator for this

- Growing mediums include soil, compost, perlite, coco coir, rockwool, vermiculite, peat moss, calcined diatomaceous earth.

- Hydroponics can be used very successfully but set up costs can be expensive

- Don't overcrowd your plants, they must be given enough space to allow free air circulation, light to reach most of their leaves and room to grow

- Use pots that drain freely

- Create a grow room workspace that makes caring for your plants easy. A cramped or poorly set out workspace will mean you and your plants will suffer

CHAPTER 3 - WATER

I mentioned water a couple of times in the previous chapter. Truth be known, water or the lack or too much thereof, is the principal cause of failure to the novice marijuana grower.

Water is a vital ingredient to practically every living thing on earth and marijuana is no exception. However, cannabis is a little bit fussy when it comes to water, it needs plenty to grow, but not so much that all of its roots are constantly sitting in it.

When the plant is germinating don't overwater, but keep the top layer of the soil moist, but not wet, this can be done twice a day with a spray bottle. When the plant produces a sprout stop spritzing and try to keep the area around the stem dry, so it doesn't rot. Water carefully around the sprout until it becomes established and remember cannabis plants hate being too wet so depending on the environment, size of the pot and growing medium you will need to judge how often the plant requires water, so it has just enough, but not too much.

Overwatering can cause plant stress as the roots cannot access enough oxygen. The younger the plant the more prone to this problem they are. It can be hard to tell if you are overwatering or underwatering as the symptoms displayed by the plant for both are exactly the same, the leaves droop and the plant looks generally unhappy. Simply test the soil with your finger to see if it feels damp, if it is then don't water the plant as there is still plenty of water available to the plant to draw from the soil. If it is dry go ahead and give the plant a good watering, making sure any run-off is removed. This is where having the right good draining growing medium and pot is of great importance, as if the soil holds too much water it will suffocate the plant.

As the plants grow, they will naturally require increasing amounts of water, but they do not like to be wet all the time. It is important to allow the plants soil to dry out quite a bit to provide aeration between watering. This means that giving a little water often is a bad idea but giving a lot of water every 2 to 3 days is a much better method.

It is normal for tap water to contain chemicals such as chlorine, which are damaging to the beneficial bacteria that grow in the soil around the plant. To help prevent the chlorine killing off the bacteria you can try adding a little sodium to the water before watering. This binds the chlorine by bonding with it creating a weak salt solution, which won't damage the plant. Most water also contains minerals, which are beneficial to the plant's growth and shouldn't cause any problems. If you are concerned about the added chemicals in your tap water, you can set up a rainwater collector and use that or a water filtration system will remove impurities.

If you don't want to hand water your plants, which can be a chore if you have a lot, then setting up a simple pipe watering system is simple and effective. A thin plastic tube is run around all our plants and into each plant pot you should have two tubes coming off the main tube into the soil to give even watering. These kinds of systems can be purchased from any good garden store and are generally not very expensive depending on what you buy. Some even have timers so you can set watering times for the entire week saving you a lot of work. But do remember to check that the level of water your plants are receiving is right for them, or problems will quickly materialize.

I cannot stress enough just how important getting the watering of your plant is if you want strong healthy productive plants.

TAKEAWAY

- During germination dampen the soil by misting twice every day

- During the growth period water heavily every 2 to 3 days and monitor the soil dampness daily

- As plants mature the frequency of watering may need to be increased to every other day

- Be careful not to overwater as it is essential the cannabis roots can get oxygen, or they will suffocate

- Use a water filter if your tap water is high in chemicals

- Don't forget to add your liquid plant feed to the water when needed

- Incorrect watering is the biggest cause of failure when growing marijuana

CHAPTER 4 – PLANTING AND GERMINATION

Once you have your grow room setup you can start planting seeds and getting them to germinate. Seeds can be planted into the large pot where the plant will spend its entire life, or alternatively into seed trays where the "plugs" once germinated and growing a healthy root system can be transplanted into their growing on pots.

Using seed trays will save time, water and electricity as you only need to focus on a small area, whereas if you plant each seed into its growing pot a lot more water, and electricity will be needed to keep the young plants growing and healthy.

In order to get your seeds to germinate you will need to give them the essential ingredients they need.

Place your seed just below the surface of the soil and keep it moist from twice daily misting for approximately 7 days. Keep them warm, but not hot. The seeds don't need light for germination, but growers often use the lights after sowing the seeds to warm the soil as this helps to promote germination. Keeping the lights on is also a good idea so they are ready for when the first sprouts appear. Although the seeds don't need light until they germinate and produce visible sprouts, bear in mind that light is their sustenance as young sprouts, and plants deprived of light at this stage may be detrimentally affected later in life. The lights should be kept close to the young sprouts and dropping them to about four inches away from the soil is the perfect height, providing the lights you are using don't generate too much heat.

You should get between 75% to 80% of the seeds to germinate, but this will depend on several factors such as the maturity of the seed, how old it is and its overall quality.

You can also try the wet kitchen towel method, which you might be familiar with if you ever grew mustard cress as a kid. Simply dampen a few sheets of paper kitchen towel placed on a plate, place the seeds onto the towel leaving a little space between each and then cover with another sheet of damp kitchen towel. You may get a greater germination rate with this method, but this is often lost due to damage when transplanting the sprouts into pots.

Garden stores will often stock kits for growing seedlings and these can be a good option for a beginner as you don't need to transplant the seedlings until they are a little more mature.

Over time you will discover your own favored method to sprout and grow on seedlings and it can be interesting to experiment with different techniques to see what works best for you.

Best Soil for Germination

You can buy special soil from garden stores called "germination soil". They are not any different to regular soils other than they don't contain any compost. The best germination soils are those with a Nitrogen, Phosphorus, Potassium (NPK) ratio of about 5:1:1 or 8:4:4, this just means 5 parts Nitrogen to 1-part Phosphorus and 1-part Potassium and so on. Nitrogen is the key ingredient in germination soils.

Transplanting

If you chose to germinate your seeds in seed trays, on kitchen paper or in small pots at some stage you will need to transplant them to their growing containers. If you leave this too long the plants may become root bound, stop growing and possibly die.

One of the problems encountered when transplanting seedlings to their growing containers is "transplant shock", to avoid this great care must be taken when transplanting seedlings. Ensure the soil is moist and that you lift the seedling very carefully, making sure not to damage it in any way, before placing it in a hole you have made in the soil of its new pot, that is just large enough to take its young root system. The seedling once placed into its growing pot should be at the same height in the soil as it was in its original growing tray or container.

Gently backfill the hole with soil and ensure that it is all well moistened so that the plants original growing media and new combine and meld together. If done correctly the plant will continue to grow happily as if nothing ever happened.

Growing Containers

As we discussed in chapter 2 you have a good choice of different containers to pick from, but as a rule of thumb remember that marijuana plants can grow an extensive root system and although small containers might be fine for germination and young seedlings, they won't be enough to grow on the maturing plant. To do this you need to choose a container that will remain adequate for much of your plant's life and I recommend a container of between 2 to 5 gallons, although the larger one is preferable, to ensure the roots have all the space they need to breathe and grow.

Other things to remember are pH balance and texture of your soil. It needs to be free draining and of pH between 6.0 and 8.0. If the soil has a muddy consistency, then insufficient oxygen will reach the roots.

TAKEAWAY

● It is easiest to plant seeds into seed trays so that as the seeds germinate each "plug" can easily be repotted.

● Seeds should be planted just below the soil

● Keep seeds warm and moist

● Light isn't necessary for germination, but will be required as soon as the seed sprouts

● It is usual for only 75% to 80% of seeds to germinate

● The easiest soil for germination is called germination soil and can be purchased from your local garden store

● When transplanting seedlings be very careful not to damage them as they are extremely delicate

● Transplant seedlings into their growing containers using the growing medium of your choice. The container should be able to hold 2 to 5 gallons of soil

● Check the soil pH regularly it should be maintained at 7

CHAPTER 5 – PLANT CARE AND GROWTH

One of the best aspects of using a grow room for your marijuana cultivation, is that it gives you a lot of control over almost every aspect of the growth process.

Lights

As your seedlings begin to mature and you have transplanted them into their growing pots you will need to adjust your lights. The lights should be kept quite close to the top of the leaves as cannabis plants require a lot of light to really thrive. A distance of between two and 6 inches should be maintained, depending on the amount of heat generated from the type of lights you are using (the hotter the lights the greater the distance), you will need to adjust the height regularly.

As the plants begin to grow, they will require around 18 hours of light each day and this will be applicable to most of the plant's life until they are ready to produce flower buds. To maintain this schedule, it is best to use a lighting timer that will automatically switch the lights on or off according to how you program it. Some lights come with a timer built in.

Light energy is essential to the health and vigor of the cannabis plant, if they don't get enough light they won't grow.

As your plants mature maintain the distance between the lights and the plants. Some lights will tell you the best distance to keep them from the plants but be sure to check that the plants leaves aren't getting burned by the light's proximity.

Soil Control

Marijuana likes nutrient rich soil with a pH or around 7.0, which is neutral. Keep a careful eye on the soil pH as a fluctuation of just one point in either direction can have significant effects of your plants. You can find pH soil testing kits online or at your local garden store.

If the soil becomes too acidic you can add a little lime to the water to adjust it back down, but don't be too heavy handed about this; do it gradually or you will tip the scale the other way.

If the soil is too alkaline you can add some cottonseed meal, coffee grounds or lemon peel. You may also be able to find an acidic fertilizer that will help lower the alkalinity if fed to the plant.

Chemical contamination is the most common cause of pH fluctuation. If your soil becomes very affected either way, it may become necessary to perform a soil flush. This means placing the affected plant in its pot under a faucet of running water to wash out the contaminants from the soil. This is a very drastic measure and should only be done when absolutely necessary. Once the plant has been flushed remove it from its pot and leave to drain for a couple of hours before adding some new soil and repotting. The biggest risk of plant flushing is that your plant's roots become overly saturated, so allowing the plant to air without its pot for a few hours can significantly help.

Vegetative Growth Stage

When your plants reach the vegetative growth stage their growth rate will increase rapidly. You will notice new leaves and branches appearing all the time and they will begin to look like proper marijuana plants. Ensure that during this stage you maintain the correct moisture levels and hours of light, room temperature, humidity and airflow. Check your plants carefully each day for any signs of problems as neglecting any aspect could be detrimental to your plant's ability to thrive and produce the best possible flower buds.

Feeding and Nutrients

pH balance continues to be of concern throughout the life of your plant, but correct nutrient balance is also of importance. Topical fertilizers can be used to dress the plants, but a better method is often to water in the nutrients by mixing them with the water given to your plants. Please note however that too many nutrients will make the soil toxic and is as bad for your plants as too few nutrients.

NPK nutrients are the three main ones required, but calcium, magnesium and sulfur (Ca, Mg and S) are also necessary during the vegetative growth stage. As with seedlings N (Nitrogen) should be at least double that of P (Phosphorus) and K (Potassium). Feeding should only be done about once per week and dilute the nutrients by 50% otherwise toxicity may occur.

You will easily be able to find plant food at your local garden store or special cannabis mixes online.

It is advisable to keep a few pre-prepared batches made up ready, one of these should include your 5:1:1 or 8:4:4 NPK solution. Another I recommend is an NPK solution where P is in the highest concentration, this is only used however during the flowering stage. Other useful solutions to have on hand are micronutrients.

Pruning

In order to help your marijuana plants, produce the highest quantity of buds for harvest, it is necessary to do a little pruning. If done right, it can be of great value to your marijuana plant and produce a higher yield.

Just hacking branches off your plants without any thought isn't the best of ideas, so I will try and teach you how it can be done correctly to increase your yields.

Some expert growers say they never prune their plants, they prefer instead to allow nature to do her job. Gentle pruning can however be very useful and when it is done correctly can get the most THC from the plant.

Pruning isn't difficult to do. It is simply cutting off pieces of your plants in order to encourage stronger healthier plants. It can be particularly advantageous when a part of the plant is already dead or has discolored leaves. The plant won't regenerate unless the injured parts are removed.

You can always expect a certain number of leaves to die off. This is perfectly normal in the plant's natural life cycle. The swift removal of these leaves can help your plant focus its resources on the healthy areas instead of wasting them on the dying ones. By clipping the stems of the dying leaves, you will be benefiting your plant and saving it unnecessary effort. Your plant can then use its energy to grow new leaves and branches and this will ultimately result in a healthier plant.

Pruning also promotes the growth of new branches and the more branches you have, the higher the yield will be when you come to harvest. Once these new branches start to sprout leaves you can remove the original leaves from which they grew. It is pointless to keep them as they will just yellow and die eventually anyway. This will provide more light to the small leaves that are lower down on the plant and encourage them to grow and produce chlorophyll.

If your plant is looking overly tall and spindly then you can take away the top and the ends of some of the branches. This stimulates new branch growth to occur and instead of one branch you will end up with two. This creates a bushier plant with more branches and more leaves. It can slow down growth, so some people prefer not to do it.

Time to Prune

You shouldn't prune your plant until after the second week of the growing phase. By this time the plant will already have some internodes and it should be easy to see how the plant is growing. Note that Indica plants grow a little more slowly that Sativas, so you might want to wait until the third week of the growing phase.

Once your plants reach flowering phase it is OK to keep pruning until the second week as during this time the plant is still growing. But don't continue to prune any later than this as the plant will need its energy for flowering.

Up until this point you can remove up to a quarter of the new side shoots each week but be careful that you leave enough old leaves in place because they have a larger leaf surface and produce sugar needed by the plant to grow.

Pruning Methods

There are several pruning methods that can be used by the novice grower, each has its own challenges and benefits. Sometimes combining methods can work too.

Topping is a technique that involves removing the top main shoot of the plant. This will result in stimulating new growth and the plant will grow new shoots and branches. If you continue to do this, the plant will eventually take on the shape of a downward facing cone. This can be beneficial as it maximizes the amount of light that the plant can receive. This technique is good if you are using a grow room as your lights will be more effective.

You can start topping your plant when you see secondary growth appearing near the low nodes as your plant is then mature enough to withstand the topping process.

Only cut the latest shoot when topping so the damage you are causing the plant is minimal. The plant will use energy to heal and this will prevent it from growing for a few days.

It is possible to top multiple times but leave enough time between each session to allow the plant to recover.

Topping is a useful practice if the height of your grow room is limited. Because Sativas can grow very rapidly and attain quite a considerable height, this method can help to keep them manageable. Because Sativas don't grow very wide, you can then have more plants in a smaller space because the light shining down onto the plant will have the most effect.

Because topping will cause your plants to produce more main buds, each individual bud will be smaller than if you hadn't topped. This can be advantageous as it makes the buds less prone to bud rot and other bud problems.

Beware of the plant becoming too top heavy as it can break under its own weight. If you notice the plant becoming very top heavy strengthen it with a support and use tape just under the topping to prevent it from splitting.

Don't top Indicas, as their growth rate is too slow.

Fimming

This is the partial removal of the latest shoot growing from the plant. It will create four main buds instead of just one. When you are fimming a plant it will become wider and less tall and will have more leaves exposed to be able to take up light.

Fimming is done by removing the top two thirds of the stem and leaves, leaving the lower stem and leaves in place. Two new shoots will then grow.

As with topping, fimming causes damage that the plant must repair, and it will slow the plants growth while it heals. Sometimes you'll also see the two newest leaves that grow are also damaged, but this is normal.

Fimming can be done several times but allow time between each session for the plant to heal. Only fim when the plant is mature enough and in its growing stage or the first week of flowering stage.

As with topping fimming can be useful to prevent plants from becoming too tall and encourages them to grow wider instead. It will also help the plant absorb light due to the increase of leaves at a higher level helping to increase the plants yield.

Also, like topping, fimming creates more, but smaller buds that are less prone to disease and bud rot. They are also liable to becoming top heavy, so taping and support may be necessary.

Fimming can be use on indoor or outdoor plants, but don't fim Indicas as they are too slow growing.

Plant Stress

Plant stress is a major underlying cause to all your marijuana growing problems, by learning about what causes plant stress, you can also learn how to avoid it. Just like people plants can become stressed from their surrounding environment. This type of stress is known as abiotic or sometimes non-living stress. Stress can also come from other living organism that cause damage or disease and this type of stress is called biotic stress.

Water stress is the most common abiotic stress suffered by all plants, not just marijuana. For a plant to grow and be healthy it requires just the right amount of water; too much and it will suffer from flooding stress, where the plant's roots become suffocated, and the cells of the plant swell and burst. On the other side of the scale is drought stress caused by either too little water or the water drying up or draining away too quickly, called desiccation. Too much or too little water can both lead to the loss of the plant, so avoiding it is the best solution.

Temperature stress is another type of stress that plants can suffer. Just like us plants dislike being either too hot or too cold. The optimal temperature is required if the plant is going to flourish and grow strong and healthy.

When temperatures fall too low, plants can get cold stress or chilling stress. If this becomes extreme, then freezing stress can occur.

Plants with cold stress find it difficult to take up enough nutrients and water. This in turn leads to cell desiccation, which starves the plant. When extremely cold temperatures occur, and the plant's cells become frozen the plant will die. Marijuana are not frost tolerant and cannot survive very cold weather.

Hot weather can be equally problematic as very intense heat will cause the proteins in the plant's cells to break down. This process is known as denaturation. The plant's cell walls can literally melt a bit like plastic melts, affecting the permeability of the plants cell membranes. This again causes the plant to not be able to take up water or nutrients efficiently. Luckily marijuana is pretty hardy against heat, but not completely heat resistant.

Other Abiotic Stressors

Wind stress can damage the plant from sheer force, by blowing the plant over or causing the stem or branches to break. Wind can also stop transpiration, which is the water moving through the plant. If transpiration cannot occur, then the plant will die due to desiccation.

Wildfires will destroy your outdoor cannabis crop, as the intense heat breaks down the plants cell structure and melts it.

Fertilizers and pesticides can also cause abiotic stress when nutritional imbalances occur and cause toxicity. If outdoor crops are grown on land that has a high level of salt, then too much salt uptake by the plant will also lead to cell desiccation. This is because the salt will draw water out of the plants cells by a process called osmosis.

Heavy metals are also a threat to plants grown outdoors. In some areas, heavy metals such as lead, chromium, arsenic, zinc, cadmium, copper, mercury and nickel are found in high concentrations in the soil. This is generally more likely in industrial areas or places where heavy agriculture has affected the natural balance of the soil. Test kits are available to check your soil for heavy metals.

Heavy metals prevent plants from being able to function normally and can affect their biochemical activities including photosynthesis.

Biotic Stress

Living organisms including insects, weeds, bacteria, fungi and viruses all cause biotic stress to plants. Fungi is the most common stressor for marijuana and there are over 8,000 species of fungi that can cause plant disease. When you compare this to the number of bacteria that can stress plants, it numbers only around 14. There are also very few pathogenic plant viruses, but they still cause a huge amount of damage.

Microorganisms can be responsible for a variety of conditions, including leaf spots, plant wilt, root rot, or seed damage. Insects can also act as virus vectors when they attack and damage a plant's leaves, stem or flowers, transferring bacteria and viruses from infected plants to healthy ones.

Weeds become a plant stressor when they overtake and push out the growth of your marijuana plants. Weeds will compete for space, nutrients and water and because they can grow extremely quickly and produce a lot of seeds it can be difficult to keep them under control.

TAKEAWAY

• Lights should be height adjustable and maintained between 2 to 6 inches away from your plants

• During the growing phase, plants require approximately 18 hours of light per day

• If plants don't receive enough light they will not flourish and grow

• Test soil pH regularly and keep it at 7

• If soil pH rises very high or drops very low, flush the plant

• Check your plants carefully each day for any signs of distress and address problems promptly

• Feed your growing plants NPK nutrients in the form of liquid plant food added to the water, by following the manufacturers instructions the feed should be in the ratio of 5:1:1, with the 5 being nitrogen

• When your plants are in flowering phase, the ratio of NPK needs to change so that the phosphorus levels are higher

• Check your plants carefully for bugs and remove any you find

• Prune your plants to encourage bush growth and to prevent them from becoming leggy

CHAPTER 6 – CLONING

The ability to clone your marijuana plants can be a useful skill. By cloning you can produce plants with identical properties to their parents and so replicate their traits. This is very advantageous if you've found the ideal plant that produces just the right combination of properties you want.

There's no need to clone your cannabis plants, as growing from seeds is fine, but seeds are inevitably a mix of their parents' genetics and many variations can occur. If you clone a plant there is zero variation, the plant will be identical to its parent.

If you like the idea of having a reliable method of ensuring your plants retain the same qualities and identical genetic code to their mother, then cloning is the best option as everything about them will be the same.

A single mother plant can produce over 50 clones every week and clone lines can be kept going for many years.

How Cloning Works

Simply put, cloning is done by taking a cutting from the mother plant and waiting for it to root, then growing it on just as you would any other marijuana plant.

In practice it is of course a little trickier than this, but with care and practice you will soon be cloning like a pro.

It is normal to use the bottom branches of your plants to use as clones as if left on the mother plant they are the least productive. The best cannabis plants to choose as mothers are between 2 and 3 months old, but any mature plant can be cloned.

You can expect to lose quite a few of your clones before they take root, it isn't unusual for only 1 in 10 to survive, so don't allow this to discourage you.

You should choose the best possible plant to be the mother. The attributes should include:

• Strong, healthy, vigorous growth

• Large roots

• Strong buds

• Great yields

Clones cut from plants at the vegetative growth stage stand a better chance of survival than those taken when the mother plant is flowering. Also, cuttings taken from a flowering plant there are other things that also need to be considered, which will be explained later.

When you have selected your mother plant you need to prepare it. To do this you must reduce the amount of nitrogen it is receiving by 10% 12 days before you take the first cutting. This will give the clone a better chance of rooting.

Using mother plants that came from feminized seeds can produce hermaphrodite clones, so it is better to only use mothers grown from regular seeds. Also, do not use autoflowering mothers as your clones will not reach maturity before flowering and this will give you a very reduced crop. Sativa strains tend to clone more easily than Indica strains, but hybrids are also a good choice.

Viruses

A mother plant needs to be free from any signs of disease before being used for cloning, as if the mother plant has any viruses they will pass onto the clones. Clones can also get viruses and if they are used to create further clones, they too will carry the virus.

The older the mother plant is, the higher the risk is that she will carry a viral infection. Younger stronger plants are a lot less susceptible to viruses that older ones. Clones' immunity to viruses is lower than its parent plant and as generations of clones are created, so immunity diminishes.

If you do notice a plant showing signs of a virus then it must be destroyed, and the area sterilized. Sterilization can be done with hydrogen peroxide.

Taking Your Cuttings

When you are ready to take your first clone cuttings you need to prepare your equipment and ensure it is sterilized correctly. Make sure you select a very sharp blade, scissors or pruners as the cut you make must be clean and crisp.

Select one of the lower branches of your mother plant that has good leaf growth. You should cut the branch about 1 inch above a couple of nodes and some leaves so that new branches can grow on the mother. You should have a cutting that is around 6 to 8 inches long. When you make the cut do it at a 45-degree angle, not just straight across the branch. This aids water absorption by the cutting. Immediately place the cut of your cutting under running water.

Growing Roots

It is best to use a soilless media to root your cutting in as it is less likely to introduce any pathogens. Cuttings require media that is loose to allow plenty of oxygen to circulate, and well-draining.

Dip the cut end of the cutting into a rooting hormone, this can be in the form of a liquid, powder or gel. In a pre-prepared container that is deep enough to allow new root growth to establish, plant your cutting 1 to 1 ½ inches below the surface of pre-dampened growing medium. Carefully place a clear plastic bag over the plant and place it somewhere where the temperature is between 55F and 75F and there is indirect lighting. Open the bag daily to allow fresh air to circulate and keep the growing media moist, spraying water is a good way to do this, just as you would with seeds and seedlings. Allow two to three weeks to pass before checking for root growth, some plants may take a little longer.

When your plant is showing strong root growth it can be repotted into a larger container to be grown on.

Baby Clone Care

While your baby clones are trying to grow roots, they will need careful care and attention. Keep their growing environment at an even temperature of between 72F and 77F, avoiding drafts if possible.

Spray the entire cutting with water several times a day, as they cannot yet absorb water through roots until they grow. Add a ¼ mix nutrient solution to the water every few days.

For roots to form you will need to give the cuttings about 18 hours of light and 6 hours of darkness each day. It is better to use lights that give off low heat to avoid burning the plants and keep them 2 to 4 inches above the plant. You can also make use of indirect sunlight coming into a room.

When the clone is well established, has grown a strong root system and has been transplanted into its growing pot, grow it on until it is well grown strong and vigorous, then you can change the lighting to bring it into flowering stage.

Cloning Females

If you wish to clone only female plants, you will need to ensure that your cutting is from a female plant that had a minimum of 4 weeks vegetative growth and was mature enough to flower.

Marijuana plants are hermaphrodites and a clone can be a different sex to the mother plant.

Keep the clones in complete darkness for at least 12 hours or more each day for 14 days. If any light reaches them during their "dark" time, the process will fail.

After the 14 days you will notice small blossoms on the cuttings. Continue the process until you can easily identify male and female plants and dispose of the males.

To return the plants to vegetative growth give them light for 48 hours uninterrupted and then you can resume normal vegetative growth light patterns.

TAKEAWAY

• Cloning creates plants that are almost identical to the mother plant

• A single mother plant can produce more than 50 clones

• Mother plants must be more than 2 months of age and in vegetative growth stage

- Only around 1 in 10 of your clones will survive

- Prepare the mother plant by reducing the nitrogen feed 12 days before taking cuttings to help improve rooting

- Don't use mothers grown from feminized seeds or from autoflowering strains

- Viruses can occur in cloned plants. Destroy any clones with signs of viruses and avoid using the same mother again

- Only use a sharp bladed instrument to take cuttings

- Make the cut at a 45-degree angle not straight across

- Place the cut of your newly cut cutting under running water to help water uptake

- Use a rooting hormone to help your cutting take root

- Mist your cutting with water several times a day. Add nutrients to the misting water at a ¼ dilution to normal (add three times more water to the feed) and feed every few days

- When your cutting has taken root carefully transfer it to its growing container

- To make female clones use only female mothers and keep your clones in darkness for at least 12 hours for 14 days. This should allow you to identify males from females

- Once you have identified the sex of your plants you can grow them on just as you would any other marijuana plant

CHAPTER 7 – PESTS AND DISEASE

Usually marijuana grown indoors doesn't suffer very much from pests or disease. However, it isn't completely impossible for your plants to become affected. The most likely problems will be from poor management and will include plants that are lacking in nutrients, which is easily remedied as described in the vegetative growth section in Chapter 5. The same is true for plants that are given too many nutrients.

Pests however are a different matter and preventing and eliminating them is a necessity, because once they are in your grow room they can quickly thrive in the warm, moist environment and decimate your crop. As with most things, prevention is most definitely better, and easier, than cure.

Pests such as mites and whitefly can be almost impossible to detect and are easily brought in from outside on your clothes or come in through a crack in your window. Mites are often present in houses without our even realizing it and although many houseplants are resistant to these types of pests your marijuana plant won't be.

To test if you have any unseen predators living in your houseplants you can perform a simple test. Take a marijuana seedling and place it next to your house plant, if your seedling starts to show signs of distress drooping leaves, change of color, lack of vitality then you probably have mites living in your home.

As a precaution avoid using any tools you use on your houseplants in your grow room. If there are any windows in your grow room, cover them with fine nylon mesh. Using pasteurized soil is also a wise precaution to prevent bringing any larva or eggs into the grow room.

If you suspect you do have a pest outbreak be sure to act immediately. Pests can be eliminated in several different ways. It is best to avoid the use of insecticides if possible as they contain chemicals that are not great for human health. You can try force flowering plants that appear to be affected if only a few plants are showing symptoms. Or try removing affected leaves. If your plants are already flowering, the pests are unlikely to cause much of a problem.

If you must resort to insecticides, look for those that are safe to use on vegetables, as these break down into safe chemical compounds such as water or CO_2. Start out by applying sparingly but accurately and remove any affected leaves prior to spraying. DO NOT apply any insecticide to plants that are flowering.

Mold, Mildew and Bud Rot

Mold, mildew and bud rot can cause serious problems and cause significant damage to your crops. There are several types of mold, which affect cannabis, but powdery mildew and bud rot are by far the most common.

Powdery Mildew leaves a thin layer of a white powder like substance on the cannabis leaves, but it can quickly take hold and infect the entire plant.

The mildew prevents the plant from being able to photosynthesize properly and starves the plant of vital light energy causing it to yellow, shrivel, brown and eventually die.

Spotting the early signs which are small white spots and treating at this stage is the best option. Once the mildew takes hold it will begin producing spores that can rapidly spread throughout the crop.

Treating mildew at an early stage can be achieved by removing any infected leaves, reducing the humidity and spraying the plant with a natural safe fungicide. Note that using a fungicide will affect the quality of your bud if done during harvest as it alters the taste, aroma and quality of your product.

A simple solution of baking soda dissolved in water can be an effective treatment if used when signs first appear.

- 1 tablespoon baking soda

- ½ teaspoon dishwashing liquid soap

- 1 gallon of water

By spraying this mixture onto the leaves of the plant you can prevent and treat mildew in its early stages, but if the mildew has taken hold it might be insufficient to treat it. Treatment should be continued every 14 days.

Bud Rot or Botrytis first attacks the base of the plant's stem and systematically spreads up through the rest of the plant. It is difficult to catch early, and thorough regular inspection of your plants is necessary if you want to stop the disease before it does too much damage.

The symptoms are characterized by the kola's leaves starting to dry and becoming withered or discolored. If you notice your plant's leaves have turned yellow overnight this can also be a symptom. You might also notice "fluff" which can be white, grey or blue-green appearing among the buds. If humidity is low the bud can even crumble at the slightest touch. If humidity is high the fluff can become more like sludge that decomposes the plant.

When bud rot is advanced you might notice black dots appearing in the mold, these are spores that will spread to other plants. They are also damaging to health if breathed in.

Young plants can also be affected, but it is less common.

Special sprays can be purchased to help minimize bud rot, but it is very difficult to cure completely.

Prevention of mildew or bud rot is a far better strategy than trying to cure the problem. To do this do not allow the temperature in your grow room to drop below 70F in order to prevent spores from spreading.

Air circulation is essential, and air must always be permitted to circulate freely around each plant. The best way of doing this and to also prevent humidity build up is by installing an exhaust fan that vents the humid air from the grow room and allows fresh air to replace it. Fungus LOVES humidity, so keep it to a minimum.

Should your plants become too bushy it makes it difficult to maintain air circulation and keep the humidity down. Reducing the amount of leaves can help to reduce this problem and the leaves you should remove are those that get the least light as they are not benefiting your plant anyway.

Bud rot tends to target your biggest, thickets, longest kolas, so keep a careful eye on them.

If you do notice any affected buds remove them immediately and dispose of where they can't contaminate other plants. If you don't act quickly you will lose your entire harvest.

One last thing is to remember the fungus spores can be transported on you, so be careful that you don't cause contamination from the clothes you are wearing.

TAKEAWAY

• Insect pests can still affect your plants indoors. Be vigilant and remove any you see immediately

• Don't use any equipment from your garden without sterilizing it first

• If you suspect you have an insect problem, act immediately

- Only use insecticides that are for use on fruits and vegetables

- Do not use insecticide on flowering plants

- To avoid problems with molds and mildew maintain good air circulation around your plants and don't allow humidity to become too high

- To prevent mildew and mold you can make a baking soda spray

- If you must resort to fungicide, ensure it is designed for use on fruits and vegetables

- Remember fungus loves humidity

Fungus spores and insects can be transported into your grow room on your clothing

CHAPTER 8 – SEXING

Although sexing your plants can be quite tricky, once you know what you are looking for it is straightforward, and the more practiced you become the easier it will get.

Marijuana plants are either male, female or hermaphrodite (both male and female at the same time). Working out which set your plants are is important if you want to maximize bud production and THC levels. Unfertilized female plants produce the goods and male or hermaphrodite plants should be removed from the room before pollination can occur. You can take pollen from your male plants if you are interested in breeding to produce seeds with certain traits.

As the plants begin to mature, they exhibit signs of their sex. The male plants start to show signs of pre-flowering before the females, usually by approximately two weeks. Male plants also start to get taller than the females and the male pre-flowers can be seen at the branch junctions. They are clearly visible to the eye and look like sacs that resemble tiny buds but are actually little pollen sacs. Male plants need to mature faster than the females in order to pollinate them they do this by dropping their pollen sacs down onto the female plants to begin pollination.

Female pre-flowers also appear at the junction between the stem and the branches and it is normal for them to start forming a fourth or fifth branch from the base of the junction, you will also see tiny white hairs called pistils.

Once these signs are visible you know the plants are ready to enter flowering stage and can remove the males.

Just because male plants don't produce a lot of THC they are not without use. They can still be smoked or used for culinary purposes to produce a slight high. It is important to be aware that if you miss just one male plant and leave it in your grow room with the females, it will pollinate them all, as one male is capable of pollinating hundreds of females.

TAKEAWAY

- You can get male, female and hermaphrodite plants

- Unfertilized female plants have the highest concentrations of THC

- Maturing plants can be sexed when they start showing signs of pre-flowering

- Male plants will pre-flower approximately two weeks before female plants

- Male pre-flowers are visible at the stem/branch junctions. They look like tiny round sacs

Female pre-flowers are visible also at the stem/branch junctions. They form extra branches and small white hairs called pistils

CHAPTER 9 – FLOWERING AND HARVESTING

One of the best parts about growing marijuana indoors, is that you get to choose when your plants come into flower.

Before inducing flowering, check and double check your plants and ensure you remove any males from the room.

Forcing Flowering

When you are sure you have removed all the male plants you are ready to begin force flowering. If you want to pollinate a few female plants in order to produce seeds to grow on, which avoids the cost of buying new seeds, then you can put them with a male once you have force flowered them.

To bring your plants to a state of flowering you need to give them 12 hours of light and then 12 hours of complete darkness. It is important that it is complete darkness and absolutely no light can enter the grow room during the 12-hour dark period. Absolutely no lights emphatically means absolutely no light, no flashlights, no cracks in the curtains, nothing but total darkness. For your plants to be ready to harvest can take anywhere from 6 weeks to as much as 5 months, although the average time is about 10 to 12 weeks.

Using a timer to switch the lights on and off for you can be very advantageous and will avoid you forgetting.

When you enter the grow room during the light phase of each day you will begin to notice that the plants are producing more branches, complete with buds and flowers. They take on a cone shape rather like a Christmas tree. The plant will now also start producing THC and you will notice the increase in aroma.

The pistils you used to identify the sex of your plants will change from white to brown, red or orange. This color change indicates that they are ripe and are ready for picking.

As your plants flower, they will naturally release moisture during the night part of their cycle. This will result in a rise in humidity, which can cause mold and mildew and can also attracts pests.

Harvesting

It is common for people to harvest too late, this causes over ripeness and can make your product smell more like cut grass. Use trichome color as your indicator of when to harvest. To do this get yourself a small hand-held microscope that is capable of magnifying to 60x to 100x. When looking at your trichomes they will look like tiny water droplets at the end of tiny shoots. By using a magnifier, you can clearly see the color of these water droplet like trichomes. When they turn from clear to milky, they are ready for harvest. If they become amber in color, they are over ripe. Trichomes that are clear are not yet mature.

• Preparation for your harvest is important. In the 14 days before you harvest stop fertilizing your plants and instead just give them distilled water or if you can't do that ordinary tap water will do. This will remove residual chemical buildups caused by the fertilizers. Your plant will have enough nutrients stored up within it to keep it healthy and by flushing them like this you will create a better tasting bud.

• Keep the plants you are going to harvest in total darkness for 48 hours prior to harvesting. This will help increase the amount of resin in the buds.

• If you want to achieve the best THC content, then you must harvest your plants in the morning.

• Remove one branch at a time by cutting it at its base with sharp pruners.

• Start by removing any of the fan leaves first and work your way along to the buds, the more leaves you remove, the faster your buds will dry.

• Hang the buds up in a warm dry place for 7 to 21 days or until the bud feels dry but not brittle. This will cure and dry the product. Being impatient at this stage will produce and inferior product.

• Other methods of curing can be read about in the outdoor growing section in chapter 15.

Manicuring is just the process of removing leaves that are growing around your bud. By carefully removing them you will be left with a tight tasty bud. By doing it as part of harvesting you will help speed up the drying process. Some people prefer to do it once the buds have been dried, but it is up to you.

How to manicure:

• Using a small pair of sharp scissors and wearing thin latex or cotton gloves hold your cut marijuana by its stem and start by removing the larger fan leaves, gradually working your way up to the bud.

• When you reach the bud trim away the leaf surrounding it as much as possible without damaging the bud itself.

• Do this on a big table or other smooth surface so clear up is easy.

• Clean off any resin residue from your scissors, or it will make your scissors blunt.

• Once manicured hang your buds by their stem to dry.

Note that harvesting marijuana can take you an entire day and it really stinks, so ensure you give yourself plenty of time and ventilation. DO NOT fall into the temptation to immediately "try" some of your freshly harvested marijuana, leave it to dry and cure and it will be a whole lot better!

TAKEAWAY

- You can choose when your indoor plants flower by adjusting their exposure to light

- Don't forget to remove any male plants from the grow room if you don't want to pollinate your females

- To induce flowering give your plants 12 hours of light and 12 hours of total darkness each day

- It can take anywhere from 6 weeks to 5 months before plants are ready to harvest

- Use a timer to switch the lights on and off for you, so you don't need to remember to do it

- As plants begin to produce buds their smell can get very strong

- Flowering plants produce more moisture, so good ventilation and humidity reduction are crucially important to prevent disease

- Buy a good hand-held magnifier that magnifies to 60x or 100x to check for maturity. This is done by looking at the buds' trichomes. These look like small water droplets on stalks. Clear trichomes mean the bud is not mature. Milky trichomes mean the bud is mature and ready for harvest. Amber trichomes mean the bud is over mature.

- Stop feeding plants 14 days prior to harvesting

- Keep plants in total darkness 48 hours before harvesting

- Harvest in the morning

- Cure and dry your plants for 7 to 21 days

- To manicure your buds, remove all leaves with a sharp knife or scissors and wear gloves!

- It takes a day to harvest your marijuana and it stinks!

SECTION TWO – OUTDOOR GROWING

CHAPTER 10 – OUTDOOR ENVIRONMENT

For people with the space and seclusion it can be preferable to grow your marijuana from seed outdoors. Not only is it more natural, but it is a lot less expensive as you won't require all the lights, heaters, vents, fans and so forth.

Outdoor growing allows your plants to flourish in a natural environment. The biggest problems are:

Your plants are visible to anyone unless you are very remotely situated. Even if your yard has high fences, once the plants mature the smell will give them away.

Soil

It doesn't matter how or where you decide to grow your cannabis plants, but what does matter is the quality of the soil you use to do it. Unfortunately, not all types of dirt are great for growing yourself a bumper crop of healthy plants, but even if the soil in your chosen spot isn't the best, there are things you can do to improve it.

The first thing you need to do is to test the soil pH using a soil testing kit to check it is within the neutral area. If it is showing as being either acidic or alkaline you can amend it using organic compost or lime and so on. See the section on soil in the indoor growing section as the techniques for soil adjustment are the same.

You will still need to give your plants some food and an NPK fertilizer with a ratio of about 5:1:1 as in indoor growing is perfect. Your plants will want mostly nitrogen until they get to the flowering stage, at which time phosphorus is the main requirement.

Light

Outdoor growing takes away the stresses of having to remember to turn lights on and off, Mother Nature does the job for you. The sun provides plenty of light for your plants and is far better than anything artificial. Sometimes problems can occur if you raise young plants indoors and then transfer them outside, because the light intensity provided by the sun is so much stronger. This can shock your plants and can kill them. It is better to sow your seeds outside in pots ready to transplant later, so that a change from artificial light to sunlight is not a problem.

If you do start your plants off indoors, then start by placing them in a lightly shaded area for the first few days, each day move them into the direct sunlight for an ever-increasing length of time until they are in it all day. You can achieve this within 7 to 10 days.

If you live in a location where you get a lot of cloud cover, your plants may not receive enough light and it could become necessary to bring them indoors at night and place them under lamps. Tall trees, building or other obstructions can also place your plants into too much shade.

When you choose your site, try to consider the light and be aware of how much is available throughout the day. If you can plant your crop on a south facing slope, then they will get a lot of light all day.

Temperature

This is something that is almost impossible to control if your plants are in the ground outdoors. If they are in pots then you could bring them inside at night if the temperature became too cold, or if it gets very hot and the roots are in danger of overheating you will need to give them a lot more water, but without allowing the roots to become waterlogged.

Weather

When plants are grown outside, they are naturally exposed to whatever weather nature throws at them, whether it be sun, wind, rain, hail, sleet or snow. Some types of weather will damage your plants. The plants are generally able to survive most of what nature sends their way providing they are strong and healthy and correctly nourished. Even if they do get damaged, they will usually heal. If you are expecting strong winds you can support your weakest plants by putting in some stakes and attaching them with a soft material (cut up ladies' pantyhose work really well). Put your stake around six inches away from the bottom of your plant and tie the plant to the stake.

If the land you want to grow your crop on doesn't have other small plants growing on it naturally, then it won't be good for growing your marijuana. Look for signs that the ground you want to grow on is fertile.

Air

Unlike the problems encountered with indoor growing, air and CO_2 are in plentiful supply in the great outdoors, so there will be no need for you to worry about this.

Humidity

There isn't a lot you can do about air humidity if you live in a particularly damp area. If you do, it is advisable to leave larger gaps between each of your plants so that air can circulate around them freely.

Site

The best possible site for your marijuana garden is on a gentle south facing slope with good loamy soil, easy access, a plentiful water supply and away from prying eyes.

TAKEAWAY

- Good quality soil is key.

- Do a pH test to check soil is 7.

- Make sure the site has access to water

- Heavy soils are the worst for growing marijuana

- Young plants raised indoors will need to be introduced to sunlight slowly over a week before planting outside

- Avoid areas with a lot of shade, such as beneath tall trees. Cannabis plants need plenty of sunlight

- Stop roots from overheating during hot periods by watering early each morning

- The best location is south facing, sunny, secluded, accessible and secure

CHAPTER 11 – SOWING AND GERMINATION OUTDOORS

Before buying seeds, it is necessary to consider your environment. It can be difficult to grow seeds that are reliant on light cycle, so getting seeds that can autoflower are far better for the outdoor grower. Buying strains that have been cross bred between cannabis ruderalis and cannabis sativa can produce autoflowering plant strains that have excellent hardiness but still have high THC or CBD levels. Using autoflowering plants can allow the grower to have multiple harvests in one season without the worry of light deprivation being required to make their plants bud. The THC levels are likely to be more in line with the plants CBD levels, but this can be beneficial as CBD negates the negative symptoms sometimes experienced by THC.

Seed Sowing

There isn't really any right or wrong when it comes to sowing your seeds. Some people like to sew them neatly in rows, while others just scatter them on top of the soil, this method is known as broadcast seeding.

A better method is to create mounds in the soil that run along in rows parallel to each other, this is called ridge and farrow seeding. You then plant the seeds on top of the mound along the ridge. The advantage to this technique is that even if the soil gets very wet it won't affect your seedlings as the water drains into the farrow. If you do use this method, or the sowing in rows method, ensure you cover the seed with enough soil to keep the seed moist. A shallow covering will be just fine.

If you need your plants to blend into their surroundings, then the broadcast method may be the best option as it will look the most natural. However, this method isn't the best one if you want to give your seeds the best chance to germinate. By covering your seeds with a little soil, it protects them, and the blanket of moist earth warms them and helps them to germinate. If you just broadcast your seeds onto the surface of the ground then they don't get this warm, moist protective layer and many more of the seeds will fail to germinate. For this reason, only use the broadcast method if you have lots of seeds and are unconcerned if many of them don't go on to grow into adult plants.

Germination

Seeds require moisture and warmth in order to germinate. This however is a fine balance as making the seeds too wet will kill them. If you use the mound method, you can add water to the farrows and the mounds will take up the water without saturating the seeds.

If the area you live in remains cool well into the spring, you might need to germinate your seeds inside. This is simple to do, and you can follow the instructions shown in the indoor growing section. Once your seedlings are well established and the weather gets warmer you can transplant them outdoors, but keep in mind that shock from sunlight can kill them, so introduce them to the sun slowly over a 7-day period.

As a reminder your ideal planting location will:

• Have naturally fertile soil

• Be on a slight south facing slope

• Have easy access to water

• Not be easily visible

At the end of the day, marijuana is a plant like any other and will grow most anywhere, but it is as well to remember that to get the best crop, it needs the best conditions

TAKEAWAY

• Autoflowering seeds can be good for outdoor growing, particularly if the area you live gets cold quickly at the end of summer

• See sowing methods include:

Broadcast where seeds are just scattered across the surface of the soil

Linear when seeds are deliberately planted in rows

Ridge and Farrow, where parallel mounds are created, and the seeds are planted in the mounds, this helps with water regulation

CHAPTER 12 – OUTDOOR WATERING

Although the chapter on watering may be short, the reason they are given their own chapters is because correct watering is SO essential to growing healthy plants.

When your plants are just little seedlings, they don't require a lot of water, just a dampening of the soil each day. But as they begin to grow and mature their water needs will grow exponentially. Without enough water they won't thrive and produce a good crop, so ensuring you can give them the water they need is essential.

Each adult plant can take up around a gallon of water each day. But by the time they are adults their root systems should be well established, and they will be able to take up most of the water they need from the surrounding soil.

Remember also that marijuana plants hate their feet (roots) to be suffocated by soil that is overly wet, as their roots require oxygen to thrive. For this reason, it is best not to water your plants each day. Instead soak them every two days for best results.

If your chosen sight hasn't got water on tap, it doesn't mean that you can't use it, it just means you will have to think of other means to get the water to your plants. If there is a nearby stream you can use buckets to transport the water. Or if there is a building rig up a water butt to save any rainwater that falls. You can even get large water containers on trailers, which you can fill up elsewhere and then tow to your growing location.

The possibility is you may not even need to give your plants much in the way of additional water if you live in an area of high rainfall.

Plants that are under watered will wilt, but this can also occur from over watering and from the heat of the sun on the leaves. To check if your plant is getting sufficient water you need to dig down into the soil to about 6 inches but be careful to avoid the roots. Using your finger as a gauge, see if the soil is moist and cool as this is a good indication that there is enough water. If the soil is warm and dry, then your plants need more water. If it is wet and cold, then they have too much.

Different types of soil will hold water for varying lengths of time. Sandy soils tend to drain quickly and don't retain a lot of water, while clay soils can easily become waterlogged. The ideal soil is a loamy one. This type of soil is light, filled with decomposed organic matter and combines both sandy and clay soils into a happy medium. You can improve soil by adding organic matter (compost), and its addition will also feed your plants as it contains nutrients.

Remember that you can add plant feed to your water to ensure that your growing plants are getting enough nitrogen and your flowering plants are getting enough phosphorus.

TAKEAWAY

• Seedlings need a gentle sprinkling of water each day to keep the surface soil damp

• More mature plants need water every couple of days, sometimes more as they mature

- Check the soil for moisture by making a 6 cm hole next to the plant, with your finger check the soil, it should be damp and cool

Different soils hold onto water in different ways:

- Sandy soils is fast draining

- Loamy soil maintains moistness but drains away excess

- Clay or heavy soil holds water and can suffocate the roots of your plants

CHAPTER 13 – PLANT CARE OUTDOORS

Unlike indoor marijuana growing outdoor plants don't need the same level of daily attention. By getting into a routine of watering and feeding if required, there isn't much else you need to worry about.

If your plants begin to look a bit leggy it could be that they are a little too close together and so are competing for light. To help this you can remove any weak plants, thus thinning the crop a little and also remove some of the foliage lower down that isn't getting much light. Cutting the top of the plant off will also cause it to branch out and can give you a lot more buds at harvest.

When you do look at your plants, observe them carefully and notice if you can see anything that might be wrong with them. Outdoor plants are a lot more vulnerable to pests and disease, so a little more vigilance is required.

Nutrient Balance

Nutrient deficiencies or excess are one of the biggest problems usually encountered when growing outdoor plants. It is a subtle balance that is required to get the best results and maintain optimum health. As we have seen before the key nutrients are Nitrogen, Phosphorus and Potassium and during the seedling and growing phases your plants will require more nitrogen at a ratio of 5:1:1.

Overfeeding your plant nutrients will have just as large a detrimental effect as underfeeding it. As a rule of thumb plants generally require feeding around once a fortnight, but it is dependent on your soil and the nutrients the plants can take from it.

If you have been feeding your plants in a balanced way it could be the pH level of the soil that has gone out of whack, test the pH levels and adjust accordingly to bring them back in line to neutral.

Sunlight can also cause problems as if the days are particularly long and hot the leaves of your plants can become burned. There isn't a lot you can do about this unfortunately.

Sometimes even though you are giving your plants nutrients at the right levels they still don't thrive. This can be because they cannot take up the nutrients correctly due to a problem with the soil. Doing a soil flush by stopping all nutrients and flushing the soil with lots of water for several days to remove all the nutrients can help. This is because an imbalance in the nutrient ratio can be the problem. Too much of one nutrient may cause the plant to become deficient in another. Once the soil has been flushed check the pH. It should be 7. Add well-rotted compost if possible and allow the plant to settle for a week. Hopefully you will see improvements as the nutrients from the compost start feeding the plant. You can then resume your NPK feeding in the water if you think it will be beneficial.

Another feeding method is called "foliar feeding", this involves adding your soluble plant food to water and placing it in a spray bottle. Spray the solution onto your plant's leaves, either first thing in the morning or in the evening when the sun has gone down. It's important that you don't wet the leaves of your plants when the sun is strong as this can cause a magnifying effect for the sun and burn the leaves of your plants.

Nitrogen Deficiency

Nitrogen is required to help your plants produce chlorophyll, an essential chemical required by the plant for photosynthesis. It also helps with amino acids, which are the elements that create proteins and are essential to keeping your plants healthy.

Nitrogen deficiency is exhibited by the older leaves on the base and middle of the plant by them turning yellow. The largest risk period for nitrogen deficiency is when your plants are flowering. The reason for this is because during this phase the plant will utilize the reserves of nutrients stored in its leaves and this can become depleted during the flowering phase.

If your plant is in the vegetation phase it is more problematic as a plant with nitrogen deficiency isn't going to grow. To remedy this, you will need to increase the nitrogen uptake as quickly as possible. The addition of blood meal, fish meal, cottonseed meal or worm manure can all help with this. You should be able to find something suitable at your local garden store or online.

Ensure you check the pH level regularly to keep it balanced.

The yellowed leaves will never re-green, they will just fall off, but your plant will soon recover, and new leaves will grow.

Phosphorus Deficiency

Phosphorus is used for growing strong healthy roots and increasing the strength in the plant's stem and leaves. It is also important during the flowering phase or for germinating seeds.

Plants that are deficient in phosphorus exhibit slow growth and may appear frail or weak. The edges of the leaves will lose the vibrant green and often brown and begin to curl inwards. It is usually easier to notice the symptoms on cold days as the cold stops the plant from being able to absorb so much phosphorus from the soil. A pH imbalance can also prevent correct phosphorus uptake.

To treat a phosphorus imbalance, you can add top dressings high in phosphorus such as bone meal, bat guano or worm castings. But the easiest solution is to apply NPK fertilizers in the water or using the misting method.

Another excellent remedy is crab shell meal. This can be harder to get hold of, but it is a very useful addition both for remedy and to add to your plants during the flowering stage.

It usually takes about a week before you begin to see improvements in your plants.

Potassium Deficiency

Potassium is needed for your plant's water respiration and circulation and to help make the plant resistant to disease. It also aids photosynthesis.

Water circulation is especially important during the plant's vegetative phase as it will keep the water moving throughout the entire plant.

Plants with potassium deficiency are slow growing and have leaves that look burned at the edges and on the tips. The plants themselves become less rigid and can be easily broken if bent. Mature leaves can take on a mottled yellow look and will eventually yellow completely and die.

The plant can absorb potassium quickly and easily and this makes the deficiency easy to fix. This can be done by adding a fertilizer containing potassium or you can add a little wood ash, sulfate of potash, kelp meal or granite dust. Results should be visible within a week.

Nitrogen, phosphorus and potassium are the key nutrients required to keep your plants healthy, but plants also require other micronutrients, which can be assisted using a good organic compost.

Weeding

Weeds can quickly overtake your young seedling and cause them to become crowded out. By far the best way of avoiding this is to hand weed daily until the plants are well established and flourishing. If you opted for a line seeding or mound seeding you can place a weed proof membrane between the plant rows, which can significantly reduce the number of weeds.

NEVER use weed killer. Some weed killers say that they are safe to use, but in my experience, it just isn't worth the risk. Not only could the weed killer kill your plants, but it will contaminate your marijuana.

As your plants mature and grow, they won't require so much, if any, weeding. This can vary depending on time of year and how much contamination there is by weeds in your soil. Weeds grow fastest between May to July.

In part 1 indoor growing we looked at plant stressors that affect both indoor and outdoor plants. Look at chapter 5 on plant care and growth to remind yourself what the different plant stressors are.

TAKEAWAY

- Prune leggy plants to encourage bushing

- Keep a close eye out for pests and diseases

- Check for nutrient deficiencies and adjust plant feed accordingly

- Check pH levels regularly

- If pH is unbalanced use an appropriate rebalancer or flush the soil

- Nitrogen deficiency signs = Older leaves at the base of the plant start turning yellow

- Phosphorus deficiency signs = Slow growth, plant becomes frail and weak, the edges of the leaves turn brown and leaves curl inwards

- Potassium deficiency signs = Slow growth, the edges and tips of the plant's leaves look burned, the plant loses rigidity, mature leaves have a mottled appearance

- Keep weeds under control – hand weeding daily is best

- Don't use a weed killer!

- Use a weed suppressing membrane to reduce the amount of weeding required

- Weeds grow fastest between May and July (late spring/early summer)

CHAPTER 14 – OUTDOOR PESTS AND DISEASE

Nature is a wonderful regulator, and although your plants stand the potential to be munched on by a lot more bugs out in the open, the fact is that due to those bugs having predators they will more often than not be kept in check.

The biggest problems come from common pests such as aphids, whitefly, spider mites, mealybugs or shield beetles (stink bugs).

Young plants are the most vulnerable to attack from pests as they are tender and undeveloped. Just a single meal from a group of munching insects could end the life of the plant. As the plant grows and matures it will become much tougher, making it less prone to attack from insects.

If you do suffer from bugs attacking your plants, there are various options available to you that can help solve the problem.

Pest Control

Insects such as ladybugs, lacewings and praying mantises are natural predators for insects that will eat your plants. It is possible to buy these insects and release them onto your plants to control any problems.

Birds can also help by eating the unwanted pests, species such as robins, martins, blue jays and chickadees are all beneficial and can be attracted to your garden by use of bird feeders, birdhouses, and pools of water where they can bathe and drink. You can also use ducks or chickens patrol your more mature plants as birds can take out many pests but will also feed on certain weeds, reducing your workload.

Other creatures that enjoy feeding on insects include lizards, frogs, toads, snakes and turtles. If you make a habitat that is appealing to them, then it isn't too tricky to encourage them to make your garden their home.

Companion Planting

Many plants have natural predator repelling properties. The THC present in marijuana is supposed to work as a natural pest repellent, but sometimes it benefits from a little help from other plants.

Garlic is one of the most repellent plants and keeps a wide range of pests out of your garden, including:

● Potato bugs

● Beetles

● Aphids

● Spider mites

● Rabbits

● Deer

Other plants that are beneficial include mint, for flea beetles and mice. Marigolds and scented geraniums also deter pests and can be planted in pots instead of directly into the ground.

Whatever companion planting you choose, it needs to be right next to the plants you are trying to protect.

Other Repellents

It is possible to create all manner of homemade sprays that can work quite effectively. One such concoction is made up of just a few ingredients:

• Liquid garlic extract

• Dish soap

• Cayenne pepper

Barriers that stop crawling insects are also effective. To do this create a solid ring of wood ash about 6 feet away from your plants. This will need renewing if it rains.

Other insect control methods include traps that attract certain insects, or even hand removal where you simply patrol your plants first thing in the morning removing any pests you see.

It isn't just insects that can be a nuisance either. Animals such as rabbits, deer, cows and even rats will enjoy a good munch on your plants. Fencing is the most obvious solution here, but it isn't always possible or practical to do. Some natural deterrents can be purchased such as bear urine, which you place around the perimeter of your garden. Depending on which animal has taken a fancy to your weed, an appropriate predator urine will need to be sourced to prevent the animals from returning.

Another useful device you can buy online is a motion activated water sprinkler. If you place this where animals enter your garden area it will detect them and spray a fast jet of water, which will help to startle them away. No electricity is needed as a device like this runs off a 9-volt battery.

Generally, as your plants mature animals will become less interested in them and the plants will be less attractive to the snacking animals.

Normally birds are not much of an issue, except when you plant seeds as crows, starlings, pigeons and sparrows are likely to come and help themselves to a tasty meal. To avoid your seeds or seedlings being eaten, you can use netting or plastic to cover them, or try making a scarecrow. Once the plants have grown a few leaves their appeal will be lost to the birds as they are not partial to marijuana. At this stage you want to encourage birds into your marijuana garden, because they will eat the pests that could damage your crop.

Diseases

We covered the most prominent diseases in the indoor growing section, but we will have a brief recap here as well as introducing you to a few other diseases you may also encounter.

As I explained in the plant care section, it can be easy to confuse disease with deficiency. These are not the same thing but can cause very similar symptoms.

Disease that is associated with humid conditions where there is too much humidity and too much water will cause stem rots. These are black or brown patches that appear on the plants stem, when you touch these areas, they will feel rotten.

If you have an affected plant remove it from the humid environment and allow the soil to dry out. Remember that you should allow the soil to dry out between each watering, which is why it isn't necessary to water every day once the plant is well established.

You can try to remove the fungi by using a soft material to gently rub the fungi away. If you cannot eradicate the problem you will have to resort to using a fungicide, but do not do this to plants once they are in the flowering stage.

Gray Mold is caused by a lack of ventilation that allows humidity to build up. You will first notice a discoloration at the tips of the plant's leaves as they turn a yellow brown color before withering completely. Next the pistil of the buds on the plant brown and the disease will cause a gray mold to appear over the upper parts of the plant. Eventually the mold will envelop the entire plant and the mold will turn into a slimy brown substance and kill it.

The best way to treat gray mold is to prevent high humidity buildup to occur, so if your plants are too tightly packed together thin out the smaller weaker ones and trim away excess leaves and growth so airflow can be more easily achieved.

Pythium is rather like gray mold in that it also develops in high humidity environments. This disease causes the lower part of the cannabis plant to rot, including the stem and even the roots. As with gray mold, increase air circulation around the plant. A chemical treatment may be required.

Mildew and Bud Rot can be hard to cure, and air circulation is the best preventative treatment. See the section in indoor growing for more information on diagnosing and treating these diseases.

With all disease, prevention is better than cure, so maintaining good air flow around your plants is a good way to help prevent the diseases occurring in the first instance.

Other diseases include viruses, which are very difficult to treat.

TAKEAWAY

- Encourage useful insects such as lacewings, ladybugs and praying mantises into your garden. They can also be purchased online, so you can release them onto your marijuana

- Encourage birds that eat bugs, such as robins, martins and blue jays

- Use ducks and chickens to keep the insect population under control

- Encourage lizards, frogs, toads, grass snakes and turtles to take up residence

- Plant garlic to deter both bugs and animals

- Plant mint to discourage flea beetles and mice

- Marigolds and scented geraniums also deter insect pests

- Homemade bug spray can be used to spray onto plants

- Create physical barriers around your garden using wood ash

- Deter animals by using the urine of their predators or motion activated water sprays. Both can be found online

- Net plants that are being raided by birds

CHAPTER 15 – FLOWERING, HARVESTING AND DRYING

Flowering

Because you have no control over the daylight reaching your plants outdoors, it is by far the easiest option to allow nature to do the transition from vegetative growth to flowering stage for you naturally. As the long daylight hours of summer begin to shorten, they will trigger the plant's own natural flowering stage.

Sometimes this isn't convenient, and it may be if you live in an area where frosts come early in the year, that you will need to use autoflowering varieties or encourage your plants to flower early. With a little ingenuity and effort, this can be achieved, what you need to do is cover your plants with a sheet of black plastic before sunset and take it off again after sunrise, so that your plants are getting the 12 hours of sunlight and the 12 hours of darkness necessary to cause flowering. You'll need to do this for about 2 weeks and your plants will start to flower so you can harvest.

Alternately it might be that you need your plants to stay in vegetative growth stage for longer. This will require the use of some powerful lamps being shone over your crop to maintain light. If you put the lights on a timer and get the lights to come on for around 10 minutes every couple of hours throughout the night, then the light pattern will be sufficiently altered to maintain the plants in the vegetative stage.

Harvesting

Harvesting outdoors isn't much different from harvesting indoors, except that when you harvest outdoors you will need to bring your harvest inside.

It is always a temptation to harvest too early but remember that you must allow the trichomes to turn from clear to milky before harvesting to the THC levels are at their most concentrated. Ensure however that you harvest before they get too amber in color as then they are past their best.

Harvesting male plants should be done early before they pollinate the females if you want to have female buds without seeds. Although the male buds aren't as good a quality as the females and don't provide the same levels of THC, they can nonetheless provide a decent harvest that is perfectly useable. As soon as you determine the sex of your plants pluck remove the male's plants from the garden completely. You will need to double check you have got them all a few times, just to be certain.

If you do want your male plants to pollinate your females to grow seeds for planting another crop, then simply leave them and harvest the entire crop together once the females are ready. This means waiting a little longer than if you were going to harvest them just for their buds as the seeds must be allowed to mature before harvesting.

When you are harvesting for seeds, then you won't get the same high levels of THC because the plant will need to be grown on for a little longer. To check if the seeds are ready open a seed sheath and look at the seeds. They should be dark brown with a marbling running over them. If they are still green, then they are not yet mature.

Seed plants will flower for around 4 to 5 weeks then new growth will suddenly appear. Wait for the flowers to start declining in production and then check your seeds until mature.

Harvesting plants is done by pulling them gently out of the ground and wetting the soil well beforehand can make this process a lot simpler. Obviously if you've grown each one in a pot then this process is easy, and you just need to tip the plant out of the pot.

From this point just follow the steps shown in chapter 9 flowering and harvesting in the indoor growing section.

When you do harvest, don't discard your fan leaves as they do contain a reasonable amount of THC, particularly when they have just been harvested. They can be dried in a couple of days and smoked or added to edibles.

Grading

Grading is simply the process of separating your plants parts by their strain, sex and parts. For example, it would be normal to keep all your sativa female top colas together and so on. Once all your harvest has been cut, graded and manicured then you can cure them to enhance the flavors of your produce.

Curing

There are several different methods of curing, these include:

- Air curing

- Flue curing

- Sweat curing

Air curing is probably the simplest but does take the longest. It requires you hang your manicured harvest in a dry room that is kept as close as possible to a constant 90F. This prevents mold development. If the weather is getting colder and wetter when you are curing, you will need to keep the air dry and warm by using a heater. This type of curing can take several weeks to complete.

Flue curing can be done by placing your harvested manicured plants into a water-tight container and placing it into a pool of water, such as a fish tank, that is maintained first at 90F until the plants start to fade and lose the green color. At this point the temperature should be raised to 100F and when all the green color is gone raised again to 115F for a day. Then turn the heat back down to 90F. This type of curing takes only about a week.

Sweat curing is the fastest method, taking around 5 days. Normally the colas and branches are stacked to around 1 and a half feet high by 2 feet wide minimum. The microbes in the stack start to cause fermentation in the plants and heat builds up. The plants start losing their color and as the plants lose their color, they should be removed from the stack to prevent mold or rot from taking hold. The removed plants are placed onto sheets or paper towels so that the excess moisture can easily be absorbed. This method is only really an option if you are harvesting very large quantities.

Drying

Once plants are cured, they must be dried as this allows the plants to be stored so they can be kept for later. Drying prevents mold growth and allows the product to be stored for a long time. If you air cure then the drying process will happen simultaneously, but additional drying time for the other curing methods needs to be added on and generally takes around 2 weeks.

You can speed up drying by using an oven or microwave, but it is far far better to wait and allow them to dry naturally.

TAKEAWAY

• Use autoflowering varieties of marijuana if you live in an area with short summers or cold autumns

• To force flower outdoor plants, you need to cover them with black plastic sheeting before sunset and take it off again after dawn. The plants must remain covered for at least 12 hours a day for several weeks

• To stop our plants from coming into flower when the days get shorter, use lights on a timer that come on and off at night

• Harvesting outdoor plants is just like indoor plants, but gently pull the entire plant out of the soil before cutting it up into its consecutive parts

• If you are growing plants for seeds, wait until the seeds are dark brown in color with marbling on them before harvesting. Green seeds are immature and won't germinate

● Grade your harvested plants by dividing them up into their component parts

● Air curing is simple and just requires hanging your harvested plant parts up in a warm, dry, airy room for one to three weeks

● Flue curing requires the use of a heated water tank and waterproof containers. The curing takes about one week, and extra time is needed for drying

● Sweat curing requires piling up large bundles of marijuana and allowing anaerobic bacteria to break it down. It takes around 5 days for this to happen, but extra time will be needed to dry the plants out

CHAPTER 16 – STORAGE AND SECURITY

Correct storage of your bud is necessary if you don't want it to degrade. The volatile oils that give the plant its aroma, flavor and natural beneficial chemicals can be degraded by exposure to light and heat. Keeping your product dry is also of the utmost importance to prevent mold.

What else can degrade your buds? Freezing and frequent handling will also damage the potency of your buds. The reason for this is that the trichomes, those little water droplet like things you looked at under a magnifier to see when your plant was ready to harvest, they can be knocked off. The trichomes give the bud a lot of its potency. Freezing makes the trichomes brittle and they fall off the bud into the container. Similarly, by over handling the bud, particularly if it is in a bag, will cause the trichomes to be brushed off the bud.

The most popular storage methods are small, dark colored glass jars, porcelain pots or dark colored bags. The dark colored glass prevents light from breaking down the volatile oils and degrading the THC. The containers need to be airtight as oxygen will also cause the bud to degrade over time. Once your buds are safely in their airtight container, keep them in the fridge or another cool dark place, and they will remain fresh and potent for a very long time.

If you are planning on keeping your buds for more than 3 months then you will need to freeze them, but this needs to be done with real care. First place them into a sealable plastic bag and gently squeeze out as much air as possible before sealing. Once sealed, place the bag inside a plastic container that has an airtight and watertight lid. Place this into the freezer and leave undisturbed until required. When you want to use the contents of the bag, simply take the container from the fridge and without opening it allow it to thaw out overnight. The next day you can remove the bag from the container and use the contents. This way the trichomes shouldn't have been knocked off the bud and by thawing before handling it is more likely that they will continue to stay attached.

Try whenever possible not to store your entire crop in one place. It may be convenient to do this, but if anything should occur you could lose the lot! So, spread it around a bit to maintain safety.

Security

When you grow cannabis outside it can attract unwanted attention. It is obvious that you should protect your growing plants from the glances of passersby. Even if you are growing your crop legally, thieves are a significant threat. It would be unfortunate and awful if you go through all the time, trouble and expenses of raising lovely healthy plants only to have them stolen right before you were going to harvest them. Don't forget that it isn't just the look of a cannabis plant that is a giveaway, but the pungent aroma. Even if people can't see your plants, they may well be able to smell them.

Oh, and one more piece of advice that I cannot emphasize strongly enough – TELL NO-ONE!

CHAPTER 17 - LEGALITY OF GROWING

One of the most pressing questions when considering growing marijuana, either for your own use or as part of a commercial venture, is its legality. In some ways, the answer is fairly straightforward. There are two countries that have legalized the growing and using of marijuana on a national level: Canada and Uruguay. If you're growing marijuana anywhere else, you are most likely engaging in an illegal activity on some level. Even in those two countries, legally growing is regulated and can only be done within certain guidelines, or with government licensing.

■ Legal in some form   ■ Inconsistently enforced

■ Decriminalized   ■ Illegal or no data

Practically speaking however, the question is quite a bit more complex, even if you do live in Canada and Uruguay. Marijuana is no longer considered, either publicly or scientifically, to be as dangerous to use as most other drugs, such as methamphetamine or heroin. At worst, it's regarded as being on the same level as alcohol or tobacco; it's not great for your health, but adults can make their own judgements. At best, marijuana has begun to be recognized for the complex and therapeutic herb that it is, and its many medicinal uses are being investigated.

As a result of that change in perception, the laws surrounding the use and growing of marijuana have begun to evolve. In many places, it now is legal, on some level, to both use and grow marijuana, and it looks as if legalization is going to become more popular as time goes on. There have already been many states and countries that have decriminalized marijuana, an intermediate step between illegal and strictly legal statuses.

Decriminalization is often confused with full legalization, but the two are not quite the same thing and there are some significant points of difference. In the case of decriminalization, possession or cultivation of marijuana is essentially ignored by law enforcement. They do not pursue users or growers of marijuana, but will still take action if they are confronted with use. In other words, if you smoke a joint in your home, no one will bother you. Smoke it on a street corner and the local police will most likely come and have a talk with you. Rather than facing arrest or jail, the police would issue fines or other lesser punishments. In many places, decriminalization has meant that marijuana users are required to attend classes on the effects of drugs and go through some sort of drug addiction treatment, rather than being sent to jail.

Marijuana cultivation and sale would be a 'gray market' after decriminalization, rather than the strictly illegal black market. Many places have decriminalized possession of small amounts, but possession of large amounts or cultivation remains illegal. Decriminalization can also take a less formal form, with possession and use being legal, but with no legal methods for obtaining marijuana. This is the case in Washington, D.C., where marijuana use has been legalized, but no system for growing or distributing legally has been created.

This is because that sort of licensing and regulation would require full legalization. When a state or country fully legalizes marijuana, it does more than simply remove criminal penalties for possessing, using, or growing it. Instead, laws governing an entirely new market have to be written, usually without the lawmakers having anything more than a vague idea of what that market should look like. This is particularly true with marijuana, as even when it is legalized, it remains a drug. That means there have to be standards for growing it, requirements for labeling, perhaps even training for the budtenders that will be selling it. Inspection schedules have to be established, inspectors designated, and standards by which they judge cultivators and retailers created.

That complexity is a part, perhaps a large part, of why legalizing marijuana is such a slow process. Even in many states where it has been officially legalized, there remains no legal way of obtaining it, as law makers are reluctant to create that sort of legal infrastructure for something that was considered a dangerous drug only a few years ago. Many are also not entirely sure how to go about it, whether it should be more like running a liquor store, or a pharmacy, or somewhere in between. In the United States, the fact that it remains illegal on a Federal level makes things even more complex.

Despite all that complexity, decriminalization and the next step, legalization, is becoming more popular. More states are taking on the challenge of creating legal markets, as it has been demonstrated to have many benefits. The marijuana market has been a gold mine for many, with it becoming a million or billion dollar industry in places where it has been legalized. In Canada, where it has been legalized on a national level, marijuana companies have even begun to be traded and find investors in the stock market. In Colorado, the booming marijuana industry has been a boon to their tax base and a stimulus to the economy.

Other benefits are less concrete, but just as important. Studies are showing that the legalization of marijuana leads to drop in the rate of opioid abuse and the use of harder, more dangerous drugs. The fears of a corresponding rise in teenage drug use have proven to be baseless.

The changing attitudes and spreading wave of legalization has both good and bad effects for the home grower. On the one hand, growing marijuana is now a legal right and not a crime in many places. On the other, with legalization comes regulations and laws regarding what can be grown, how you can grow it, and where. In general, the rules for growing marijuana legally are fairly easy to understand, simply giving a number of plants that it is legal to grow.

In places where marijuana has been decriminalized but not fully legalized, things can be more complex. Cultivation may be fully illegal, decriminalized up to a certain number of plants, or illegal but with rarely enforced penalties. This is a more nebulous and chancy arena, which depends on local attitudes and the opinion of the officials in charge of enforcing laws against marijuana. As these opinions change with the people holding those offices, and what may have been tolerated at one point may suddenly find you in trouble.

To make understanding the situation in your area as easy as possible, you can find a breakdown of the laws in your area, including how much you can grow and any other restrictions that may apply in the following sections.

As a note, the situation surrounding the laws on growing marijuana is constantly evolving. The guidelines we have here should be a starting place for your understanding and it would be a good idea to investigate the current state of things where you live.

Growing in the United States

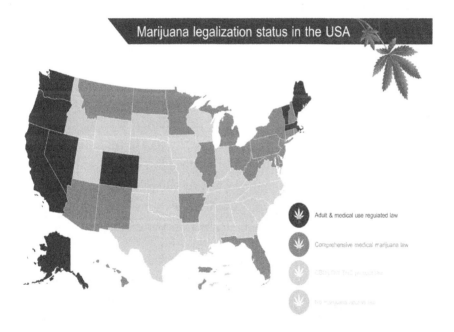

To say that the legal questions surrounding growing marijuana in the United States are complex is a profound understatement. Federally, marijuana is still considered a Schedule 1 drug, meaning that it is considered dangerous and of no medical value. Obviously, that classification is out of date. There are many movements to reclassify marijuana and update its legal status, so that may change in the near future. However, as it stands any possession or growing of marijuana is considered a crime by the Federal government.

However, it has been legalized on a state level in many areas. That leaves marijuana in a gray area, at once both legal and illegal. President Obama issued a memo instructing the justice department to not spend resources on prosecuting marijuana growers, sellers, and users in states where it had been legalized. That policy was rescinded under President Trump's administration, though the actual enforcement of laws is up to the U.S. Attorneys for each jurisdiction, most of whom have not shown any inclination toward prosecution. While that's great news and has allowed for many people to find relief in marijuana use, as well as the growth of a billion dollar industry, it's a policy that can be changed at any moment, essentially on a whim. Until there are Federal laws legalizing marijuana, growing and possessing it remains a crime.

Don't let that kill your buzz, though. On balance, it is more likely that marijuana will be fully legalized and there won't be an issue. Polling has shown 62% of Americans in favor of legalization of some sort, which is a significant majority. If you happen to live where marijuana is legal on a state level, you can grow it and use it, and even sell it with the proper licenses, without worrying too much about its Federal status.

In the United States, there are currently nine states where it is legal to grow marijuana in your home for your own consumption. There are a further nine that allow you to grow if you have some sort of medical approval. Note that even if marijuana *use* may be legal, marijuana *growing* may not be, as is true, for example, in Washington state.

Here are the states where growing for personal use is legal, with a general outline of their laws.

Alaska: If you're over the age of 21, you can grow up to six plants, though no more than three of them may be mature at any time.

California: Adults over the age of 21 can grow up to six plants, with any or all of them being mature at any one time. That limit is the same for medical card holders, though in some cases special permission to grow more may be given.

Colorado: Any adult can grow up to six plants, with up to three being mature enough to produce usable marijuana at any one time. A single residence can have up to 12 plants, no matter the number of residents living there.

District of Columbia: Adults over 21 in D.C. can also grow up to six plants, with no more than three of them being mature at once.

Maine: Each resident of the state can grow up to six fully mature plants, 12 immature plants, and any number of seedlings.

Massachusetts: Each resident of the state can grow up to six plants for personal use, with a limit of 12 plants per household. Additional plants can be grown by medical card holders with special permission.

Michigan: A resident can grow up to 12 plants for personal use.

Nevada: Residents can grow for personal use in the Silver State, but only if they are at least 25 miles from the nearest commercial dispensary. At that point, you can grow six plants, with a cap of 12 per household. Medical users can grow up to 12 plants for personal use if they live more than 25 miles from the nearest retail store.

Oregon: A resident of Oregon can grow up to four plants per household for recreational use, while a medical user can grow up to six plants. If you're a caregiver growing for the use of a patient, you can grow up to six plants per patient, but for no more than four patients at once.

All of these states require that the growing be done someplace out of public view, and usually in a locked facility. That's just generally a good idea, though, so it shouldn't be too much of a hardship.

Here are the states where it is legal to grow only if you're a registered medicinal user of marijuana. In some states, that allowance extends to folks helping the medicinal user as a caregiver, to allow for those who may benefit from marijuana use, but aren't up to the somewhat complex project of growing it themselves.

Arizona: A qualifying patient or caregiver can grow up to 12 plants if they live more than 25 miles from the nearest retail dispensary.

Hawaii: In Hawaii, a medical user can grow up to 10 plants, though they must grow in their home or someplace they own or control. Not too long ago, it was legal for caregivers to grow on patients' behalf, but a revision to the law removed that allowance.

New Mexico: Medical users can apply for a license that would allow them to grow up to four mature plants and 12 seedlings at any one time.

North Dakota: If you live more than 40 miles from a dispensary and are a registered medical user, you can grow up to eight plants. However, the growing location has to be at least 1000 ft from a public school, and you have to inform local law enforcement, among other things.

Oklahoma: Medical patients can grow up to 12 plants, with up to six being mature at any one time.

Rhode Island: A licensed medical user or their caregiver can grow up to 12 mature marijuana plants.

Vermont: Medical users or their caregivers can grow 2 mature marijuana plants, and up to 7 immature plants.

Washington: A qualifying patient can grow up to six plants for personal use, with more allowable under certain circumstances.

States that allow recreational use, as well as some states that allow medical use, also allow growing marijuana as a commercial venture. Growing as a business requires licensing, however. These licenses are complex and it's a good idea to get legal help when filling out the application. They are also expensive, costing tens or hundreds of thousands of dollars.

The competition for licenses is also *fierce* in most places. Marijuana growing and retailing has become a multi-million dollar business in Colorado, Oregon, and other places it has been legalized for recreational uses. Many people see the current market as a chance to cash in and make their fortune, or as a way to get in on the ground floor of an entirely new, growing, and legal business.

Some states are fairly liberal with licensing, giving them to many businesses, like Oregon. Others are licensing only a few growers in their state, so that many entrepreneurs are going away empty-handed.

There can be many other factors to consider if you'd like to enter the marijuana business. For example, some states are requiring the same business grow, process, and handle the retail of their marijuana, requiring a much larger initial investment. Because marijuana is still considered a Schedule 1 drug by the Federal government, most banks and credit card companies won't work with marijuana businesses. That means everything has to be run on an entirely cash basis.

Before jumping into commercial marijuana growing, it's a good idea to get some expert advice to help sort out all these issues. Luckily, there is a growing group of professional marijuana business consultants, as well as lawyers who have begun specializing in marijuana law.

Growing in Canada

Canada has joined Uruguay in legalizing marijuana use for all adults on a national level, making it the second country to do so. The national law is fairly loose, putting a cap on personal possession at 30 grams, and making it illegal to drive under the influence. Using the national law as a guideline, each province has written their own laws to handle other issues like age restrictions and growing allowances.

Most provinces are allowing users to grow for their personal use. Commercial growing is a more complex issue. In some provinces, only a Crown corporation, essentially a state-run business, will be allowed to grow and sell marijuana. Every grower will require licensing, in any case.

The licensing process in Canada, like in the U.S., can be fairly complicated. For quite a while after marijuana was legal, there was a shortage of legal marijuana because the process of licensing growers and sellers takes so long. Marijuana business in Canada does have a few advantages that makes it simpler than in the U.S. For example, Canada allows marijuana, marijuana seeds, and paraphernalia to be sold over the internet. Legalization also means Canadian marijuana businesses can use the banking system, take credit and debit card payments, transfer money electronically, and so forth.

The laws for personal growing, however, are fairly straightforward. Here are the different laws for each province.

Alberta: Adults over 18 can grow up to four plants in their home.

British Columbia: Adults over 19 can grow up to four plants in their home for personal use.

Manitoba: Growing marijuana is currently not legal in Manitoba, though there are exceptions for registered medical users.

New Brunswick: Adults over 19 can grow up to four plants for personal use.

Newfoundland and Labrador: If you're 19 or older, it is legal for you to grow four plants in your home.

Ontario: Anyone over 19 can grow up to four plants for personal use.

Prince Edward Island: Adults over the age of 19 can grow four plants.

Quebec: Growing your own marijuana is not legal in Quebec.

Saskatchewan: For anyone over 19 years old, it is legal to grow up to four marijuana plants.

Yukon: If you are over 19, you can grow up to four plants for your own use.

As with states where growing is legal in the U.S., plants have to be out of the public view, and usually must be somewhere that can be locked. Some provinces specifically require growers keep plants out of reach of children, which is certainly a wise precaution in any case.

The bottleneck in licensing has made it difficult for some users to obtain seeds to begin growing their own. There are only a couple of hundred retail locations currently open in the whole of Canada. In the Yukon territory, for example, there is only a single physical dispensary currently open. However, as it is legal to buy and sell over the internet, there are online retailers who will sell seeds, cuttings, and other supplies.

It will be exciting to see how marijuana laws, and the business side of things, evolves in Canada. It's the first large, industrial country to take such a sweeping step and there's no question many people will be watching to see how it plays out.

Growing in Mexico

Mexico is in an interesting position when it comes to legal marijuana. On the one hand, there are still laws on the books making its growing, selling, and use illegal. However, in October of 2018, Mexico's Supreme Court ruled that these laws are unconstitutional, violating the Mexican Constitutional right to personal development. This is the fifth time the court has reached this decision, which in Mexican law is a magic number. Once the same decision has been reached five times, it sets a new precedent in Mexican law, so that now prosecution for recreational use of marijuana is considered unconstitutional.

That isn't the same thing as saying it's legal in Mexico. It's closer to saying its decriminalized, an intermediate step on the way to legalization. It is still possible for someone to be arrested and prosecuted for marijuana related offenses, but the person accused could then challenge the constitutionality of that prosecution and likely win. That makes the only laws governing the use of marijuana in Mexico unenforceable.

Theoretically, the Mexican government had 90 days to create legislation legalizing marijuana, though that deadline has passed. 90 days is probably an unreasonably short amount of time to produce laws surrounding a whole new sector of business from scratch, in any case.

Only ⅓ of Mexican citizens were in favor of legalizing marijuana only a short while ago. For many reasons, Mexicans are generally against legalization. However, there have been many people watching the experiments in legalization in the U.S. and seeing the effect it has had on black market drugs and drug dealing. The war on drugs has had a devastating effect on many places in Mexico, and legalization is seen as a way to begin taking steps toward resolving those problems.

At any rate, the legal status of marijuana in Mexico remains unclear.

Growing in Europe

In general, Europe is considered to be more liberal than the United States. Whether that's true or not, their marijuana legislation is usually clearer and more unified than the U.S.'s current legal limbo.

In many places in Europe, medicinal use of marijuana is fully legal, while recreational use has been decriminalized for small amounts. Other countries still have laws against the use of marijuana, but rarely enforce them. Growing marijuana is a more complex issue, and in most countries it remains illegal, or legal only for certain regulated growers. Here's an overview of the legal status in a few European countries.

Austria: The possession of marijuana for personal use was decriminalized, though it has not been fully legalized for recreational use. Some drugs derived from cannabis are legal.

Belgium: In Belgium, possession of 3 ½ grams or less has been decriminalized. It is also legal to cultivate a single plant for personal use. Some cannabis derived drugs are legal.

Czech Republic: The possession of 10 grams or 5 plants has been decriminalized. Marijuana use for treating medical conditions is fully legal for registered patients.

Denmark: Possession and growing are still illegal, though medical use has been legalized.

France: Marijuana is still illegal in France, with only a few marijuana derived drugs being legalized at the moment.

Germany: Marijuana is illegal, but enforcement of the laws are spotty. Prosecution is optional for small amounts, but what qualifies is not specified. Users may not face prosecution, but could have drivers' licenses suspended or face some other punishment short of a court case. Growing remains illegal, though medical use for registered patients is legal. That permission is given in only rare cases, however.

Greece: Recreational use and growing are both illegal. Medical use is technically legal, though no system for registration or supply has been implemented as yet.

The Netherlands: We've all heard that marijuana is legal in Amsterdam, but the situation is a little more complex than that. For years, recreational use has been tolerated in some coffee houses, but was still illegal. A few years ago it was decriminalized for amounts less five grams, or the cultivation of up to five plants. The only place to buy it even semi-legally is still those few coffee shops, and while you won't be prosecuted for possession, your stash may be confiscated.

Portugal: Portugal was the first country to decriminalize the possession and use of marijuana, up to 25 grams of flower, along with most other illegal drugs. Medical use is also legalized, but the country has yet to take the next step of fully legalizing marijuana use. Growing marijuana remains illegal, however.

Spain: In Spain the legal situation is complex. One Spanish state, Catalonia, legalized recreational use, but the law was struck down by the national government. Public use is strictly illegal as is the sale of marijuana. However, privately growing and possession are considered misdemeanors and often overlooked. Cannabis social clubs have popped up, where people work together to grow the plants and share the crop, bypassing the laws against selling marijuana.

United Kingdom: Recreational use and growing of marijuana remain completely illegal. It has been legalized in a few cases for very specific medical conditions, such as epilepsy and for managing the more severe side effects of chemotherapy.

Though initially taking some of the first steps in decriminalizing marijuana use and growing, the countries of Europe have not followed up with full legalization. In some countries, it is still strictly prosecuted.

Growing in Central and South America

Central and South America have for decades been the front lines in the war on drugs. As a result, for many years marijuana was completely illegal, largely due to pressure for the United States government. In recent years, however, countries have begun to follow the trend of decriminalizing marijuana and allowing its use in some medical cases.

Here's an overview of laws regarding marijuana use and growing in Central and South America.

Argentina: The possession of small amounts for personal use has been decriminalized. Medical use has also been legalized.

Belize: Marijuana is illegal in this Central American country, though it is generally tolerated, and there are plans to decriminalize possession of less than 10 grams.

Bolivia: Marijuana remains illegal in Bolivia, though the growing and use of it is actually fairly widespread. Possession of less than 50 grams is decriminalized, though users may face rehabilitation and treatment for drug addiction.

Brazil: Possession of marijuana is illegal in Brazil, though small amounts will only get you community service and education on the effects of drugs. Growing or possessing more than 50 grams is considered possession and is a more serious matter.

Chile: Growing for personal use has been decriminalized, and commercial growing for the medical market is legal, subject to licensing by the government.

Colombia: Personal use has been decriminalized, as has the cultivation of up to 20 plants. Growers can't be prosecuted as long as they are only growing for personal use.

Costa Rica: This famous vacation country still has laws against the use and growing of marijuana. However, these laws are rarely if ever enforced and use is widespread throughout the country.

Ecuador: Possession of less than 10 grams has been decriminalized. Anything under that amount is not punished, though marijuana technically remains illegal. Growing is illegal.

El Salvador: Possession and growing of marijuana is illegal.

Peru: Possession of less than eight grams is not punished. Those caught cultivating marijuana, however, can face stiff prison sentences.

Uruguay: Uruguay was the first country to fully legalize marijuana and in 2017 it was the first country to sell marijuana through state owned pharmacies. In the years since, however, the marijuana industry has begun to lag behind due to a lack of political will. Growers in Uruguay have also faced problems with international financial system and banks unwillingness to do business with marijuana businesses. As a result, despite legal ways of obtaining marijuana, many people have returned to the illegal black market. The marijuana available from the black market is also considered to be stronger and of higher quality. Legal cultivation is limited to licensed growers, so no home growing in Uruguay.

CONCLUSION

Growing your own marijuana can be fun and rewarding, but don't think it will be cheap, particularly if you plan to grow indoors. The setup of a high quality and high performance grow room can run into thousands of dollars. Like any crop, sometimes you will have success, but sometimes you will also suffer failure.

Before buying anything, do your research, preparation is important and can save you from unnecessary expense down the line. Always buy the best equipment and tools you can afford, as buying cheap is often a false economy in the long term.

Growing indoors will give you a lot of control over the conditions your plants are kept in, and will keep them away from prying eyes, but the setup and care involved is far greater than if you chose to use an outdoor garden to grow your cannabis.

Be aware also that growing a good crop isn't something that happens in a couple of weeks, it takes months of hard work and dedication, paying close attention to detail and acting swiftly when problems occur.

Thank you very much for reading this Marijuana grow guide. I know this information will help you grow higher quality Marijuana and maximize your yields.

Happy Growing!

Finally, if you enjoyed this book, then I would like to ask you for a favor. Would you be kind enough to leave a review for this book on Amazon? It would be greatly appreciated.

Click here to leave a review for this book on Amazon

Take care and best regards,

Terry Gordon

REFERENCES

http://www.ilovegrowingmarijuana.com/how-to-make-marijuana-clones/

http://www.kindgreenbuds.com/cannabis-grow-bible/caring-for-outdoor-plants/

https://www.growweedeasy.com/whats-the-best-cannabis-growing-medium

https://www.growweedeasy.com/choose-right-pot

https://howtogrowmarijuana.com/marijuana-sexing/

https://cannabis.net/blog/how-to/how-to-prevent-mold-in-your-cannabis-grow

https://grow-marijuana.com/harvesting

https://www.thoughtco.com/plant-stresses-abiotic-and-biotic-stresses-419223

http://www.ilovegrowingmarijuana.com/pruning/

https://www.cannabisbusinesstimes.com/article/state-state-guide-marijuana-application-licensing-fees/

https://www.cannabisbusinesstimes.com/article/11-tips-for-winning-a-marijuana-cultivation-license/

https://www.leafly.com/news/cannabis-101/home-cannabis-cultivation-laws-a-state-by-state-guide

https://en.wikipedia.org/wiki/Legality_of_cannabis

https://www.forbes.com/sites/andrebourque/2019/01/08/canadas-cannabis-laws-by-province-and-5-burning-questions-for-2019/#5b91ecf74eb3

https://globalnews.ca/news/4619096/grow-your-own-marijuana-canada-legal/

https://en.wikipedia.org/wiki/Cannabis_in_Canada

https://en.wikipedia.org/wiki/Cannabis_laws_of_Canada_by_province_or_territory

https://legislature.maine.gov/9419

https://en.wikipedia.org/wiki/Cannabis_in_Mexico

https://www.rollingstone.com/culture/culture-news/mexico-marijuana-legal-decriminalize-pot-weed-751030/

https://www.nanalyze.com/2018/11/weed-legal-mexico/

https://www.washingtonpost.com/business/2018/11/01/mexicos-supreme-court-overturns-countrys-recreational-marijuana-ban/?noredirect=on&utm_term=.bo6737a22edb

https://elpais.com/elpais/2018/10/16/inenglish/1539687522_144922.html

Made in United States
North Haven, CT
09 June 2022

20032182R00065